Intellectual Property Rights Demystified

New Delhi – 110 034

ABOUT THE EDITORS

Dr.Mu.Ramkumar, is a faculty member of the Department of Geology, Periyar University, Salem. After completing B.Sc. Degree from National College, Bharathidasan University, Tiruchirapalli and M.Sc. degree from Annamalai University, Chidambaram, he had worked for Ph.D. program in the School of Earth Sciences, Bharathidasan University, Tiruchirapalli, under the supervision of revered teacher Prof.V.A.Chandrasekaran, on carbonate sedimentology. He has completed Post Graduate Diploma in Personnel Management and Labor Legislation from Alagappa University, Karaikudi.

Since completion of Ph.D. degree in the year 1995, he has worked in many national and international institutions viz., IIT-Kharagpur, IIT-Bombay, Andhra University and Karlsruhe University, Germany, before taking up teaching career at Periyar University. His research interests include integrated sequence and chemostratigraphy, depositional and diagenetic modeling for petroleum exploration and reservoir characterization, environmental conditions across K/T boundary, natural disaster management, modeling deltaic evolution, coastal zone management, effluent dissemination capacity of estuaries, etc. In all these fields, he has published more than 100 articles in national and international journals. He has authored two books on computers. His research works have been and are being supported financially by Alexander Von Humboldt Foundation, Germany, Department of Science and Technology, New Delhi, Council of Scientific and Industrial Research, New Delhi, University Grants Commission, New Delhi and Oil and Natural Gas Corporation, Dehra Dun. He is a recipient of Humboldt Fellowship, CSIR Research Associateship, CSIR Pool Officer Award, Young Scientist Award (twice) and was nominated for S.S.Merh Award. He is a member and honorary fellow of various scientific bodies. His name has been included in "World's who's Who" - "Emerging leaders of the World" directories compiled by Biographic Institute, U.S.A.

Dr.A.Jayakumar, is currently working as Reader and Head of the Department of Commerce, Periyar University, Salem. He has a long illustrious teaching and research career. Before joining Periyar University, he had worked for more than two decades in D.G. Vaishnav College, Chennai. His research specializations are Finance and Organizational Behavior. Four books titled "Banking and Financial System", "Business Organization and Management", "Income Tax Law and Practice" and "Income Tax Theory Law and Practice" were authored by him. Currently he is working on a book entitled "Direct Taxes". Currently he is guiding 8 Ph.D. Scholars and 2 M.Phil. Scholars. More than 25 Scholars supervised by him were awarded M.Phil. Degrees by Madras/ Periyar University in regular stream. He has also presented papers in more than 40 Seminars/Conferences/Workshops.

He has published several articles of national importance in reputed journals. He is also a life member of Indian accounting association, Tamil Nadu Investors Association and Joint-Secretary, e-com.net. He has conducted several programs on personality development. He is a member of board of studies in various Universities and autonomous colleges.

Intellectual Property Rights Demystified

Editors

Mu. RAMKUMAR, M.Sc., Ph.D., PGDPM & L.L.
Department of Geology

&

A. JAYAKUMAR, M.Com., M.Phill., Ph.D.
Head, Department of Commerce

Periyar University, Salem, Tamil Nadu, India

New Delhi – 110 034

A Paperback Division of

NEW INDIA PUBLISHING AGENCY

101, Vikas Surya Plaza, CU Block, LSC Market
Pitam Pura, New Delhi 110 034, India
Phone: + 91 (11) 27 34 17 17 Fax: + 91 (11) 27 34 16 16
Email: info@nipabooks.com
Web: www.nipabooks.com

Feedback at feedbacks@nipabooks.com

ISBN: 978-81-89422-87-5

Composed and Designed by NIPA

Foreword

The world's economy is increasingly propelled by knowledge and skills of the mind. Innovation and creativity are helping biotechnology, telecommunications and other high technology companies to achieve rapid growth. Non-innovative and non-creative companies are often left in their wake.

The United States Patent and Trademark Office (USPTO) is modernizing and improving its patent and trademark processing systems through its Strategic Plan in order to serve the needs of the world's innovators. Although it is currently the largest and possibly the most productive patent office in the world, it is hiring more than 1,000 Patent Examiners per year to keep up with its rapid increase in patent filings. Japan has developed a far-reaching national intellectual property strategy that addresses protection and enforcement issues. The European Union has adopted advanced regulations for intellectual property enforcement, among other reforms.

India, China, Brazil and other developing countries are joining developed countries in improving their systems for intellectual property protection and enforcement in order to take advantage of their knowledge capital.

India is undergoing rapid economic growth. In the year 2006, India's gross domestic product grew at more than 9%. High technology sectors accounted for a large portion of this growth. With India's growth in high technology came a corresponding increase in patent and trademark applications. The 2005 Patent Amendments, making pharmaceutical products patentable for the first time since 1970, have also contributed to a significant increase in patent applications.

The World Intellectual Property Organization has just appointed India as an International Searching and Preliminary Examining Authority under the Patent Cooperation Treaty (PCT). As a result, the Office of the Controller General of Patents, Designs and Trademarks (OCG) may be faced with unprecedented increase in the number of patent applications. In addition, a bill to accede to the Madrid Protocol has been introduced into Parliament. Accession to this Protocol could significantly increase the number of trademark applications that are examined by the OCG.

In order to improve processing and otherwise address the challenges that may arise from a significant increase in patent and trademark filings, the Indian government has invested more than $100 million in OCG infrastructure by creating new facilities in Delhi, Mumbai, Kolkata and Chennai. The Indian government is preparing to undertake a second stage of infrastructure investment, which may include hiring and training new Examiners, as well as improving information technology infrastructure and search systems.

This growth is not limited to foreign companies filing in India. Although only 20% of patent filings at the OCG are from Indian applicants, there has been a significant increase in the number of domestic applications. In addition, Indian applicants are increasingly filing for intellectual property protection overseas. In USPTO, for example, Indian origin patent applications increased by almost 25% between 2005 and 2006.

According to the World Bank, approximately two-thirds of India's population works directly or indirectly in agriculture. A similar portion of the population earns less than $2 per day. Only 10% of the workforce has formal jobs. Furthermore, only 10-15% of general college graduates are considered to be suitable for employment due to poor educational resources.

Although intellectual property cannot directly solve these problems, it can create value out of the creativity and intellect possessed by different sectors of the Indian economy. Furthermore, it will continue to boost the overall economy, which will create opportunities for the underprivileged.

Under Secretary Dudas, on behalf of the United States Patent and Trademark Office (USPTO), and Secretary Dua, on behalf of the Office of the Controller General of Patents, Designs and Trademarks (OCG), signed a Memorandum of Understanding on Bilateral Cooperation (MOU) in January 2007. The MOU includes OCG automation, modernization of intellectual property offices, development of databases, exchange of best practices on patent examination procedures, t raining of personnel, as well as collaboration on seminars and workshops for stakeholders.

The Parties signed an Action Plan to carry forward the terms of the MOU. Under the terms of the Action Plan, high-level judicial and administrative officials are participating in USPTO's Global Intellectual Property Academy. In addition, USPTO and OCG have engaged in India-based discussions and exchanges, including those on electronic filing of patents and trademarks, as well as the protection of traditional knowledge and genetic resources. Furthermore, USPTO and OCG are undertaking a comprehensive series of public outreach programs that are bringing a message of intellectual property and how it may be protected and enforced to those in India who have had little or no exposure to it in the past.

This is just one example of bilateral cooperation that the Indian government has undertaken in order to enhance its ability to protect and enforce intellectual property. OCG has also signed MOU's on Bilateral Cooperation with the European Patent Office, the Japanese Patent Office, the UK Patent Office and the French Patent Office. Some of these MOU's are also being implemented.

President Bush and Prime Minister Singh issued a Joint Statement on March 2, 2006 in Delhi to work together to promote innovation, creativity and technological advancement by providing a vibrant intellectual property regime. The three areas for cooperation that were identified in the statement were capacity building, human resource development and public awareness programs. In furtherance of the Joint Statement, the Parties agreed to "develop a relationship of mutual trust, respect and common values in the areas of capacity building, human resource development and public awareness programs in intellectual property." The U.S. Embassy, New Delhi has embarked on sensitizing the professionals and personnel of corporate houses on IPR systems through conductance of workshops in four metros of India in cooperation with regional commerce chambers. The workshop conducted by the editors of this book to create awareness on IPR systems and laws is also an example in this direction, targeting the academics and scientists. The book covers many aspects of IPR starting from elementary concepts, evolutionary history, functions, structure and mandate of important organizations concerned with protection of IP and current scenario of IPR, which may serve as a baseline information source for beginners as wells as working professionals in the area of IPR. While provision of papers on IPR management and suggestions for creation of increased awareness on IPR are in tune with need-of-the-hour, inclusion of suitable forms for filing application towards copyrights, patents, etc., in this book as annexure would benefit the readers. The authors and the editors of this book are to be lauded for their effort in presenting a concise, yet information packed papers as an authoritative source on IPR systems, laws and practices in a simple language, understandable by all sections of the society, be it students or working professionals.

The key to advancing India's prosperity through intellectual property is public outreach. Crafts people, farmers, artists, geoscientists, small business people, professors, students and others must learn what intellectual property is and how they may utilize it. This book would be a valuable guide in fulfilling this task of creating awareness on IPR.

DOMINIC KEATING
First Secretary for Intellectual Property
United States of America Embassy, New Delhi

Preface

Studies have shown that there is a perfect link between strong IPR regime protected by rule of law and economic development of a country. India is still at nascent stage when compared with the IPR regimes of developed economies. Hence, governmental and intergovernmental initiatives in association with commerce and industrial bodies are being taken up for creating awareness on IPR. Even though the researchers of software, pharmaceutical and biomedical fields are leading the pack of most number of patent applications, requirement of such awareness in other fields is felt necessary. Based on this necessity, Dr.Mu.Ramkumar conceived an idea to conduct a workshop for geoscientists in particular, researchers in general. Response to this clarion call has been overwhelming from all quarters namely, co-shouldering the conductance of workshop by Dr.A.Jayakumar, administrative and other supports from the University authorities, financial grants from CSIR, TNSCST, KMB Granites and Periyar University, lending physical and mental labour by faculty members and research scholars of the Departments of Geology and Commerce, etc.

The conductance of workshop on IPR for geoscientists in Periyar University, Salem, is apt in atleast two major counts. First, the Salem district, wherein the Periyar University is located is considered to be the mineral belt of Tamil Nadu State. The second is, as the motto of Periyar University is *Knowledge Maketh the World,* and thus it is apt that the Periyar University conducted the workshop on IPR for geoscientists.

While there was large crowd of geoscientists who wanted to attend the workshop, there was demand from practicing lawyers and teachers and research scholars of other branches of science as well. Sensing the demand for information on IPR among people of all walks of life, the organizers of the workshop have decided to publish the lectures delivered during the workshop after peer reviewing, making the wealth of knowledge on IPR easily available and accessible to one and all. This volume is the result of such effort.

Papers in this volume provide insights on IPR right from basics to IPR management. Although the editors would not agree with all the views expressed in the papers, editors have extended the freedom of expression enshrined in our constitution not only in sprit but also in letter, principally to allow the reader to know prevailing trends in IPR, enforcement of IPR and management of IPR. If this volume motivates the readers to file for patents for their innovative ideas/designs/concepts or disseminate information on IPR and facilitates filing of patents/copyright, then the purpose of publication of this volume is well served.

Mu. RAMKUMAR
A. JAYAKUMAR

Acknowledgements

This volume contains collection of papers presented in a National Workshop sponsored by Council of Scientific and Industrial Research, New Delhi, Tamil Nadu State Council for Science and Technology, Chennai, and NSIC, New Delhi. Financial grant from these funding agencies is thankfully acknowledged. Former Vice-Chancellor of Periyar University, Prof.Dr.T.Balakrishnan, is thanked for his administrative and moral support during whose tenure the National Workshop GEO-IPR'2006 was organized by the editors of this volume. Equally important is our Honorable Vice-Chancellor Prof.Dr.M.Thangaraju, without whose administrative support, this volume would not have seen light of the day. Dr.G.Kunasekaran, Registrar i/c, and other authorities of the university, faculty members and other staff of departments of geology and commerce were of much help through offering suggestions and also for taking up important tasks for the conduct of the workshop, whose helps made the workshop successful.

Many individuals, either directly or indirectly and either in their official capacity or as a goodwill gesture helped the conveners in organizing this workshop. Although this list may be endless, the Principal of Central Law College, Salem, Prof.Manohar, Department of International Law, Dr.Ambedkar Law University, Chennai, Prof.Gopalakrishnan, IPR Chair, School of Legal Studies, Cochin University of Science and Technology, Cochin, Prof.V.A.Chandrasekaran, Professor and Head (Retd.), Department of Geology and Prof.K.Kumarasamy, Department of Geography, Bharathidasan University, Tiruchirapalli and Shri.Ifthikar, KMB Granites, Salem, are prominent.

We thank the resource persons, who, through enlightening lectures have made the workshop fruitful and beneficial to the participants and the organizers. The research scholars and students of the departments of geology and commerce were readily available for taking care of many tasks pertaining to the workshop.

The reviewers, who choose to remain anonymous, are thanked profusely for having helped the editors in the task of separating chaff from grains without altering the style and content of the papers. New India Publishing Agency, New Delhi are thanked for printing this volume on time.

Mu. RAMKUMAR
A. JAYAKUMAR

Content

Foreword *v*
Preface *ix*
Acknowledgements *xi*

1. Understanding Intellectual Property Rights (IPR) is the Need of The Hour for Geoscientists 1-9
Mu. Ramkumar, A. Jayakumar and R. Suresh

2. Nature and Scope of Intellectual Property Rights 11-24
C. C. Subha

3. Review on Recent Developments in Registration of Inventions and Protection of IPR in India 25-39
T. Poongodi Vijayakumar and Mu. Ramkumar

4. An Introduction to Patenting System of India 41-44
V.A.Ambigapathy

5. Copyright Laws of India - An Introduction 45-54
V. Thillaikumar and S. Gayathri

6. World Intellectual Property Organization (WIPO) and its Role in Promotion and Protection of IPR 55-62
M. A. Thamizh Selvi

7. Historical Evolution of Intellectual Property Protection and the Road to TRIPS 63-76
Prabha S. Nair

8. TRIPS and its Implementation on IPR Regimes of Developed and Developing Nations – An Overview 77-96
T. Agitha Gopalakrishnan

9. IPR in the Era of Globalization 97-103
A. Jahitha Begum and M. Vakkil

10. Impact of Enforcement of IPR on Developing Countries 105-112
A. Vinayagamoorthy

11. Issues and Implications of IPR – A Review 113-127
T. Ramakrishna

12. Current and Future trends of Intellectual Property Rights Management and Governance 129-139
R. Subramaniya Bharathy

13. Protection of Biogeoresources 141-146
A. Rajanikanth

14. Suggested Course of Action for Familiarization of IPR 147-150
Mu. Ramkumar, A. Jayakumar, K. Anbarasu, R. Suresh and T. Poongodi Vijayakumar

15. Annexure 151-171

Intellectual Property Rights Demystified, 2008
Mu. Ramkumar & A. Jayakumar (ed.), pp. 1-9
New India Publishing Agency, New Delhi (India)
E-mail : newindiapublishingagency@gmail.com
Web: www.bookfactoryindia.com

1

Understanding Intellectual Property Rights (IPR) is the Need of The Hour for Geoscientists

***Mu.RAMKUMAR, *A.JAYAKUMAR AND *R.SURESH**
*Department of Geology, *Department of Commerce, Periyar University, Salem - 636 011.

ABSTRACT

Concomitant with paradigm shift from agrarian and brick and mortar economy to knowledge and service based economy, India needs to adhere to the international conventions for the benefit of enriching its knowledgebase with which economic development and social welfare could be achieved. Although geoscientific research has been at the forefront and contributed immensely to our country's economic development, number of applications for patents, copyrights, etc., on geoscientific concepts, databases, innovations, designs or processes has been negligible when compared with other branches of science. This paper intends drawing the attention of geoscientists on this lacuna and provides information on fundamental aspects of IPR that may be of help to geoscientists whose innovations are waiting to be filed for patents or copyright.

INTRODUCTION

In an article appeared in Current Science, Dr.R.A.Mashelkar, Director General of Council of Scientific and Industrial Research

(CSIR), New Delhi, noted that, "the twenty first century could be termed as the century of knowledge. Innovation is the key for the production as well as processing of knowledge. A nation's ability to convert knowledge into wealth and social good through the process of innovation will determine its future; due to which, issues of generation, valuation, protection and utilization of intellectual property (IP) are going to become important all around the World. As far as the third world countries are concerned, the development of skills and competence to manage Intellectual Property Rights (IPR) are more critical. An ideal regime of IPR strikes a balance between private incentives for innovators and the public interest for maximizing access to the fruits of innovation" (Mashelkar, 2001). In this context, this paper is an attempt to enthuse the scientists in general, the geoscientists in particular to document their research innovations in appropriate for their personal benefit as well as economic development of our country.

WHY SHOULD THE GEOSCIENTISTS BE AWARE OF IPR?

While widely accepted in western culture, the status of IP is disputed in many developing nations including India. While the IPR regime could benefit the industrialized countries, the ancient civilizations that have rich cultural and traditional knowledge do not attach much importance to exclusivist nature of invention or designs. However, with the open market and globalization of economy, these countries are bound to loose not only the impetus required for keeping up with developed economies, but also to preserve their traditional knowledge, that are being patented by none other than the so-called developed countries, who attempt to patent the traditional knowledge of third world countries, claim exclusive rights for the knowledge not originally created by them and sell the very same knowledge to the very nations that possessed it since time immemorial. When the original creators point out this irony, the onus of proving it is imposed on the very nation itself, not on the stealer! Typical cases are the claims made by U.S.A. over basmati rice, healing property of turmeric, pesticide characters of neem, etc. India was able to reclaim its rights on these cases only after protracted battle in intellectual arena and legal avenues, etc, and that too due to the hilarious efforts of CSIR, backed up by Indian government and also after spending millions of dollars.

To alleviate this recurrent problem, measures such as documentation of medicinal characteristics of Indian herbs, traditional practice, etc. have been initiated by central governmental directive as a national mission. In addition, a specific mechanism, aid in filing of international patents, national patent registry have all been established and these efforts of the governmental agencies have started paying off in terms of increase in number of patents filed by Indians, research institutions and corporate.

However, it is felt that the geoscientists inclusive of academic, industrial or administrative personnel, lack the awareness at a level that exists among the medical and software fraternity. India is endowed with rich mineral deposits and has dedicated geoscientists working on various fields of mineral exploration, enrichment and judicial utilization of the natural resources. The processes, designs and ideas towards these tasks created by them are not being filed for patents, simply for the reasons that either the geoscientists are not fully aware of the importance of patents, or not realizing the necessity to claim property rights.

This attitude is not going to serve the cause of economic prosperity of our nation and hence it is high time, the geoscientists of our country are made aware of the importance of IPR and hence this paper attempts to present a ready reference for elementary aspects of IPR.

KEY DEFINITIONS

According to WIPO (World Intellectual Property Organization), intellectual property refers to creations of the mind, inventions, literary and artistic work, symbols, names, images and designs used in commerce. The term "Intellectual rights" has its origin from French "*droits intellectuels*" and offers protection similar to that of rights of ownership over physical property. The term "intellectual property" originated in Europe during the 19th century. A French author used the term "*propriйtй intellectuelle*" in his book published in the year 1846. Modern usage of Intellectual Property Rights (IPR) includes proprietorship to the creator for original inventions, designs, trademarks, processes and concepts to provide economic incentives. Intellectual property rights such as copyrights and patents give the holder an exclusive right to sell, or license, the right to use that work. IPR is classified into three (but not limited to) major categories namely, copyright (that covers creative works and expressions of ideas), patent (that covers ideas with industrial and other applications) and trademark (that covers means to uniquely identify a producer or other source of reputation). This exclusive right over such intellectual property granted by governments is limited for a fixed term of time duration, which in turn can be renewed for successive time duration.

The copyrights for items like literary, musical and artistic works like songs, musical scores, poetry, paintings, sculpture, films, architecture, maps, technical drawings; computer programs, data base etc are provided to the creators. Copyrights provide exclusive right to the creator to use or authorize others to use his/her works. Once granted, reproduction in various forms, copying, printing, recording, public performance or adaptation are prohibited without explicit permission of the copyright holder.

An invention is defined as a process or a product, which provides a new way of doing something or provides a new solution to a problem. The patents protect inventions. The owner of inventions can get his/her invention registered under a patent. A patent is granted for a fixed period from the date of filing the application.

A trademark can be patented like inventions and industrial designs. The trademark can be combination of words, letters, numbers, drawings, images, symbols, and even sounds. The trademarks not only protect the owner rights but also causes the consumer to have confidence in the product purchased. The reputation and the quality are also associated with trademarks. The trademarks are generally registered for seven years but can be renewed indefinitely by applying again and paying required fee.

IPR ORGANIZATIONS AND LAWS

WTO (World Trade Organization) is the organization that oversees multilateral commerce. IPC (International Patent Classification) assigns unique code to each patent and forms basis for patent search by national patent offices. TRIPS (Trade Related Intellectual Property Rights) is the agreement subscribed by all the signatory nations of WTO. WIPO is an organization under United Nations, works on promoting human intellect (Mashelkar, 2001). Intellectual Property Rights Appellate Board (IPAB) is the competent authority for alleviating grievances emanating from patent rights.

India has an exclusive act for granting IPR namely, Patents Act, 1970 amended effective from January 1, 1995. There is another act namely, the Patents Rules act 1972 amended effective from June 2, 1999. After subscribing to the international treaties namely "Convention of WIPO" and TRIPS Agreement under the World Trade Organization and the Paris Convention for the protection of Industrial Property with effect from 7th December' 1998 and Patent Cooperation Treaty (PCT) with effective from 7th December' 1998, Indian government enacted a simplified and comprehensive Patents (Amendment) Rules 2006.

In India, patent applications are examined and granted by decentralized Patent offices, located in different cities (Table.1) and working under the control of the Ministry of Commerce and Industry. As per these laws, an invention means any new and useful art, process, method or manner of manufacture; machine, apparatus or other article; or substance produced by manufacture and includes any new and useful improvement of any of them and an alleged invention. In compliance to the TRIPS agreement, India has Trademarks Act 1999 and the Trademarks Rules 2002 to provide level playing field for national and international brand owners.

CAN GEOSCIENTISTS APPLY FOR PATENT OR CLAIM FOR COPYRIGHT OR IPR?

Gone are the days geologists ventured for field survey with clinometer, toposheet, scribbling pad, pencil and a jacob's staff and searched for landmarks to locate themselves on the basemap. Now, modern day geology student walks to the field with "Magallen™"/ "Garmin™" GPS that contains preloaded field map, records field observations in "Casio™" personal digital diary or scribbles on "Sony™" or "Panasonic™" Palmtop, takes field photographs by "Nokia™" N series mobile and sends it immediately to his Research Supervisor sitting at laboratory located far away via MMS (Multimedia Messaging Service) for getting clarification/opinion, it is time to understand how far the copyrighted/patented/trademarked world influences a routine geological field work. And it is also time, geoscientists raise to the occasion in claiming copyright/IPR and patents her/his innovations.

Table 1. Patent offices and their jurisdiction

S.No.	Patent Office	Jurisdiction
1	Patent Office Branch, Mumbai.	Gujrat, Goa, Maharashtra, Madhya Pradesh and the Union Territories of Daman & Diu and Dadra & Nagar Haveli.
2	Patent Office Branch, New Delhi.	Haryana, Himachal Pradesh, Jammu & Kashmir, Punjab, Rajasthan, Uttar Pradesh and Delhi and the Union Territory of Chandigarh.
3	Patent Office Branch, Chennai.	Andhra Pradesh, Karnataka, Kerala, Tamilnadu and Pondicherry and the Union Territories of Laccadive, Minicoy and Aminidivi Islands.
4	Patent Office Kolkata (Head Office)	Rest of India

Unlike research pursuits in pharma, biotechnology or software development fields, geoscientific research in India is largely funded by governmental agencies and private participation is negligible. In addition, almost all the geoscientists who work on developing equipments for sampling and mining, innovative concepts, designs, mineral processing/beneficiation methods and many other commercially usable aspects, stop at publishing their results in reputed journals while the thumb rule of IPR suggests that never publish your results before applying for patent! Pharmaceutical research has shown a strong link between R&D and IPR and patent protection (Commission on Intellectual Property Rights Study Paper 2b authored by Kettler and Collins). As geoscience essentially deals with mineral wealth, directly linked to economic development, inculcation of the culture of filing for patents/copyright/IPR by geoscientists would certainly match well with other branches of sciences. Establishment of such culture and demonstration of link between R&D in geoscience and economic incentives would also encourage private participation, which in turn would augment increased flow of private funding for geoscience research. The IPR Commission report cited above noted that many studies have demonstrated the link between patents and Innovation. Hence, filing for patents by geoscientists would help improve our economy.

HOW AND WHERE TO APPLY FOR IPR?

Application has to be made at the nearest patent office in triplicate. The term nearest patent office denotes normal residence of the applicant or the work place from where the actual invention originated. Provisional application can also be made, but it must be followed by complete application within 12-15 months from the date of filing provisional application. Applications must enclose an abstract of the invention, an undertaking on filing date and number and information on the status of foreign patent application, necessary drawings if applicable and a Demand draft/cheque for application fee. According to the recent amendments of patent rules 2006, application fee can be paid through electronic payment mode also. Komal Shah (2006) stressed that not only applying for patent is important, but also a skillfully drafted patent, taking into consideration both the technical and legal aspects. According to this author, technical requirements demand a clear understanding on invention, the patentable aspects, the distinguishing features over previous work and the language that best describes the invention. The patent application requires sound understanding on international patent law, failing which, even if the patent is granted, it would be more of a liability.

Applications are examined critically at the patent office and objections if any, are communicated to the author/inventor and then the application can be suitably modified by the applicant and resubmitted within 15 months from the date of first examination report, failing which it is deemed that the applicant has withdrawn the application. If suitably amended and resubmitted, it will be published in Gazette.

Any contender, who wishes to challenge the patent application, can file his/her contention through serving notice within four months of publication in Gazette. If there is no contention, a patent number is provided and entered in patent register followed by granting of exclusive patent right over the invention to the applicant. Normally, this exclusive right is granted for a period of 14 years from the date of filing complete application. On expiry of this term, exclusive right can be claimed by making a request and paying prescribed renewal fee.

WHAT THE GEOSCIENTISTS REQUIRE IN THE ERA OF INTELLECTUAL PROPERTY RIGHTS?

The non-availability of explicit protection under the existing patent/copyright laws for *mineral beneficiation processes/ Prototype Models of Exploration and Exploitation* is a serious impediment for the geoscientists. Offering such protection would encourage geoscientists, professional organizations and private companies to embark upon research in utilization of low-grade ores, bringing in added economic development and optimal utilization of natural resources available in India, which may reduce dependence on imports in the long run. Hence, the continuing process of legal reforms in conformity with WTO and TRIPS agreements by the federal government may consider offering legal protection for mineral beneficiation process, which may be treated at par with pharmacological formulation.

The voluminous data being generated by the geoscientific community pertaining to micro-scale lithology, economic mineral deposits, reserves of medium-minor scale commercially viable ore deposits, etc, that may help in establishing Small-Medium Industrial units for local area development, but in turn are not readily available to the end-users is yet another impediment and has to be alleviated through systematic documentation and collation of such data. Prerequisites for such endeavor are to digitize such data in a common format, register for copyright and to distribute data to end-users. Hence, establishment of a geological data registry by appropriate governmental agencies similar to the lines of TKDL (Traditional Knowledge Digital Library), which can form as a core repository for geological data generated by researchers and academicians is necessary. Any private agency/industry that wishes to utilize the data may pay a nominal fee depending on commercial utility value of the data. The funds so collected may be utilized for fostering geoscience education/research in India, besides making the geoscience data registry self-supporting and autonomous. Similar lines of data registry can be established for other branches of sciences too.

Acknowledgements

This paper was presented during the National workshop on "Geosciences, Georesources and IPR Regime: Familiarization and Practice". Council of Scientific and Industrial Research, New Delhi, Tamil Nadu State Council for Science and Technology, Chennai have sponsored the event. Moral, academic and administrative supports from Prof.Dr.T.Balakrishnan, the Former Vice-Chancellor of Periyar University, Salem, made conductance of the workshop successfully and publication of this paper possible.

References

Mashelkar, R.A., 2001 Intellectual Property Rights and the Third World. Current science, v.81. pp.955-965.

Shah, K., 2006 Deft drafting key to prefect patents. Business Line dated 01.09.2006.

Intellectual Property Rights Demystified, 2008
Mu. Ramkumar & A. Jayakumar (ed.), pp. 11-24
New India Publishing Agency, New Delhi (India)
E-mail : newindiapublishingagency@gmail.com
Web: www.bookfactoryindia.com

2

Nature and Scope of Intellectual Property Rights

C. C. SUBHA
Central Law College, Salem.

ABSTRACT

The law of intellectual property has assumed utmost importance the World over, in the recent past and it is being considered as one of the most important subjects of law in view of its implications on economic, social and cultural realms. The term "intellectual property" has come to be internationally recognized as covering, patents, industrial designs, copyrights, trademarks, know-how and confidential information or trade secrets. This paper presents an overview on nature and scope of these elements of IPR.

INTRODUCTION

Property may be divided into two categories namely corporeal and incorporeal property. Corporeal property is related to physical entities while incorporeal property is related to immaterial entities (e.g. patents, copyright and trademarks etc). In other words, incorporeal property is called intellectual property. Intellectual property in its literal sense means the things, which emanate from the intellectual labour of human being.

Intellectual property laws confer a bundle of exclusive rights in relation to the particular form or manner in which ideas or information are expressed or manifested and not in relation to the ideas or concepts themselves. It is therefore important to note that the term "intellectual property" denotes the specific legal rights, which authors and inventors may hold and exercise and not the intellectual work itself. Intellectual property law covers the areas of Copyright, Trademark, Patents, Geographical indication, Industrial design, Moral rights, Personality rights, Plant breeders rights, Trade dress, Trade secret, Traditional knowledge, Domain name, etc.

FEATURES OF IPR

Copyright

Copyright is a right, which gives exclusive rights to the creator for his/her original and artistic work. Copyright is in effect a right to prevent appropriation of expressed results of the labors of an author by other persons. The right is regarded as a "natural right" on the ground that nothing is more certainly a man's property than the fruit of his brain. Others regard it as not a natural right but a right conferred by the state in order to promote and encourage the labors of authors. A work is entitled for copyright protection even if it is considered bad and even if it fails to serve the purpose, for which it was intended.

The law governing copyright in India is the Copyright Act 1957. Basic features of the Act confined to the provisions of Berne convention 1886 and Universal copyright convention 1952 which were revised at Paris in 1971. This act has been amended in the years 1983, 1984, 1992, 1994 and 1999. The copyright laws of almost all countries provide protection of the following types of works.

- Literary,
- Musical works,
- Artistic works,
- Maps and technical drawings,

- Photographic works,
- Motion pictures or cinematographic works,
- Computer programs and
- Applied arts.

The different rights conferred by copyright law are :

- Reproduction rights,
- Performing rights,
- Recording rights,
- Motion picture rights,
- Broadcasting rights,
- Translation and adaptation rights and Moral rights.

It should be emphasized that copyright comes into force without registration or other formalities. So the question of applying for protection does not arise. The general philosophy of copyright is that whoever takes the initiative in creating the work makes the investment and takes financial risk to produce it, should be allowed to reap benefit.

Trademark

Trade Marks are visible signs, which distinguish the goods and services of an enterprise from those of their competitors. The term 'visible sign' covers a whole lot of things. It includes any of the following or combinations thereof.

- Arbitrary or fanciful designations,
- Names,
- Existing and invented words,
- Slogans,
- Devices,
- Numbers and their combinations,
- Letters,

- Pictures and Symbols,
- Labels and
- Combinations or arrangements of colors.

A Trade Mark has several functions. Few important functions are given below.

- A Trade Mark usually represents certain standard of quality and uniformity to consumers.
- A Trade Mark enables the manufacturer to identify goods manufactured.
- Once a mark acquires certain reputation, it enables its owner to penetrate new markets.

For getting a trademark legally protected, it has to be registered in the trademark register of the intellectual property office. International registration with the International Bureau of WIPO can also be obtained if the enterprise has its head quarters in a country, which is a party to the Madrid Agreement on international registration of marks.

After the Hindu and Mughal periods came the British regime and hence India – like other Common Wealth Countries, had to follow the British Principles of trade marks. Use of Trade Marks law started in U.K. during 15th Century. Since then, many changes were found necessary in Trade Marks laws of U.K. and thereafter in British India. Thus U.K. Merchandise Marks Act 1875 was ultimately changed into the Trade Marks Act 1938. On this basis, Indian Trade Marks Act 1940 was passed. Based on Ayyengar Committee's Report to the Govt. of India, Trade and Merchandise Marks Act 1958 was assented to by the President of India on 17.10.58 which read with the Trade and Merchandise Marks Rules 1959 to regulate Trade Marks Law and Practice in our country. The Trade Marks Act, 1999 has been enacted to amend and consolidate the law relating to trade marks. It is more compliant with the Trade Related Intellectual Property Rights (TRIPS) Agreement. Salient new features of this act are as listed herein.

- Providing for registration of trademarks for services, in addition to goods.
- Providing an Appellate board for speedy disposal of appeals.
- Providing enhanced punishment for the offences relating to trade marks.
- Filing of a single application for registration in more than one class of goods or services.
- Increasing the period of registration and renewal from 7 to 10 years.
- The person claiming to be the owner of the trademark must apply to the Registrar in the prescribed manner. The application has to be made to the Trade Mark Registry within whose territorial limits the principal place of business of the applicant is located.
- An application shall not be made in respect of goods comprised in more than one prescribed class of goods.
- On filing of the application, the authorities conduct a search to ensure that the proposed trademark is not similar or deceptively similar to existing and registered trademarks.
- Thereafter, the Registrar may accept or refuse the application, subject to any amendment/modification/ condition/limitation, as may deemed to be.
- Upon receipt and acceptance of the registration application, the Registrar shall cause the application advertised in the prescribed manner.
- If no opposition to the application is received (within generally three months from the date of the application), or if the opposition is decided in favor of the applicant, the Registrar shall register the Trade Mark.
- Registration of the Trade Mark is not compulsory. However, without the registration the owner of the Trademark cannot bring an action for infringement of trademark if other copies it.

- Application of any false trademark or trade description to any goods or the act of sale or possession of such falsely applied or used trademark constitutes a criminal offence. The punishment for various offences can be in the form of imprisonment for a period of six months to three years along with penalty at the prescribed rates. The law also provides for enhanced penalty for repetitive conviction.

Patent

Patent means a statutory grant of Exclusive right to a person/ an entity or a corporate house to exploit his/her/their/its inventions for a limited period. Invention in this regard means any new and useful

- Art, process, method or manner of manufacture.
- Machine, apparatus or other article.
- Substances produced by manufacture and including any new and useful improvement of existing one and an alleged invention.

Exclusivity of right implies that no one else can make, use, manufacture or market the invention without the consent of the patent holder. The patent right is territorial in nature. To become eligible for this right, a claim for patent must satisfy the following conditions.

- Novelty,
- Inventiveness (non-obviousness) and
- Usefulness.

However, even if an invention satisfies these conditions, section 3 of the Indian Patents Act lists the following as exceptions on which grounds, patent right may be refused.

- An invention which is frivolous or which claims anything obviously contrary to well established natural laws e.g. different types of perpetual motion machine.

- An invention whose primary or intended use of which would be contrary to law or morality or injurious to public health.
- The mere discovery of a scientific principle or the formulation of an abstract theory.
- The mere discovery of any new property or new use of known substances or the mere use of a known process, machine or apparatus unless such a known process results in a product or employs atleast one new reactant.
- A substance obtained by a mere admixture resulting only in the aggregation of the properties of the components thereof or a process for producing such substance.
- The mere arrangement, rearrangement or duplication of features of known devices each functioning independently of one another in a known way.
- A method or process of testing applicable during the process of manufacture for rendering the machine, apparatus or other equipment more efficient.
- A method of agriculture or horticulture.
- Any process for medical surgical curative, prophylactic or other treatment of human beings or any process for a similar treatment of animals or plants.
- Inventions relating to atomic energy.

Geographical Indications

A geographical indication (GI) is a name or sign used on certain products corresponding to a specific geographical location of origin. Few examples in this regard are: Uttukuli Butter, Gangeyam Bull, Rajapalaiyam hunter dogs, Madurai Jasmine flower and Tirunelveli Halwa. The use of a GI may act as a certification that the product possesses certain qualities, or enjoys a certain reputation, due to its geographical origin. Two international treaties, viz., Paris Convention for the Protection of Industrial Property, 1883 and the Madrid Agreement for the Repression of false indications of origin 1891 deal with indication of source and indication of origin respectively, whereas the Lisbon Agreement for the protection of Appellations of Origin and their international Registration, 1958 deals with appellation of origin. The TRIPS Agreement also uses the expression geographical indications. After becoming party to TRIPS agreement, India had enacted specific provisions in its legal system to protect GI.

Industrial Design

The theoretical basis for the protection of designs is similar to that of copyright. Designs are identified and recognized as a form of IP. Designs were first protected in India along with patents by patents and Designs Protection Act, 1872. This was consolidated in 1883. When patent and Design Act, 1911 was passed, separate provisions were also included to protect designs. The Design Act 2000 has come on the statute book in India in tune with TRIPS Agreement. Section 4 of the new Act has added that a design should be new, original and not been disclosed to the public in India or in any other country to enjoy the protection. The Act of 1911 did not provide for publication of design, but under new law, design can be published as soon as they are registered. Now law has provision for restoration of lapsed designs. Although designs are protected on the same as that of copyrights there are differences as listed herein.

Copyright Law	Industrial Design
Protection is purely concerned with aesthetic creations.	A design must be applied to utilitarian articles in order to be protected.
The protection subsists without formalities. Registration is not necessary.	The protection is lost unless the applicant registers it before publication or public use.
Copyright lasts in most countries for the life of the author and 50-60 years after his/her death.	Industrial design protection endures generally for a short period, say for example 7 years.

Industrial design refers to the creative activity of achieving a formal or ornamental appearance for items produced industrially. For legal protection, an industrial design must be new and original. The document certifying the protection of an industrial design is called registration certificate or a patent.

Moral Rights

Moral rights are special rights conferred on authors in addition to the economic rights. Article 6 of Berne convention confers on authors the moral rights distinguished from economic right. The moral rights are: the right to claim authorship of the work and the right to object any distortion or other modification of the work, which would be prejudicial to the author's honor or reputation.

Section 57 of the Indian Copyright Act 1957 provides such moral or special rights to the author. The rights conferred upon the authors in the Indian Copyright Act 1957 are more protective and in confirmation with the International Conventions.

Personality Rights

Personality rights consist of two types of rights, namely,

- The rights to publicity or to keep one's image and likeness from being commercially exploited without permission or contractual compensation, which is similar to the use of a trade mark and the right to privacy,
- The right to be left alone and not to permit imitate one's personality publicly without consent.

Plant Breeder's Rights

Plant breeder's rights, also known as plant variety right (PVR), are intellectual property rights granted to the breeder of a new variety of plant. The rights permit the breeder to control the seed of a new variety and the right to collect royalties for a number of years for utilizing the seed. This right guarantees income for the breeder to cover the costs of research and development. The purchase of protected varieties gives farmers the benefits of superior varieties. In return, farmers are expected to pay a small royalty, included in the purchase price, and not to sell the seed they produce. Farmers may store the production in their own bins for their own use as seed, but further sales for propagation purposes is not allowed without the written approval of the breeder. Violations of Plant Breeder's Rights can result in litigation and court–ordered restitution to the breeder.

Plant breeder's rights contain a wider array of exceptions than the general regime of patent law. Commonly, there is a defense for farm – saved seed. There is also scope for compulsory licensing to allow public access to new varieties.

The enactment of the protection of plant varieties and Farmer's Rights Act was to provide for the establishment of an effective system for protection of plant varieties. It was in compliance with India's commitment towards Agreement on Trade Related Intellectual Property Rights (TRIPS) particularly for giving effect to its Article 27 (3) (b) whereby members shall provide for the protection of plant varieties either by patents or by on effective *sui generis* system or by any combination thereof.

Trade Dress

Trade dress refers to characteristics of the visual appearance of a product or its packaging (or even the facade of a building such as a restaurant) that may be registered and protected from being used by competitors in the manner of a trade mark. These characteristics can include the three-dimensional shape, graphic design, color, or even smell of a product and/or its packaging. There are two basic requirements that must be met for trade dress protection. Those features must be capable of functioning as a source indicator – identifying either a particular product and/or its maker to consumers.

Trade Secret

Trade secret is a formula, practice, process, design, instrument, pattern, or compilation of information used by a business to obtain advantage over competitors within the same industry or profession. In some jurisdictions, such secrets are referred to as "confidential information" while in others they are a subset or example of confidential information. A company can protect its confidential information through non-compete non-disclosure contracts with its employees.

The precise language by which a trade secret is defined varies by jurisdiction (as do the particular types of information that are subject to trade secret protection). However, there are three factors that (though subject to differing interpretations) are common to all such definitions. A trade secret is some sort of information that:

- Confers some sort of economic benefit on its holder (where this benefit must derive specifically from its not being generally known, not just from the value of the information itself);
- Is the subject of reasonable efforts to maintain its secrecy and
- Is not generally known to the public.

Law does not protect trade secrets in the same manner as trademark or patents. Probably one of the most significant differences is that a trade secret is protected without disclosure of the secret.

Traditional Knowledge

Traditional knowledge (TK), indigenous knowledge (IK), and local knowledge generally refer to the matured longstanding traditions and practices of certain regional, indigenous, or local communities. Traditional knowledge also encompasses the wisdom and teachings of these communities. In many cases, traditional knowledge has been orally passed for generations from person to person. Some forms of traditional knowledge are expressed through stories, legends, folklore, rituals, songs, and even laws. Such knowledge typically distinguishes one community from another. In a sense, it becomes their "identity". For some communities, traditional knowledge takes a personal and spiritual meaning. Traditional knowledge can also reflect a community's interests. Some communities even depend on their traditional knowledge for survival. Subsequently, communities argue that traditional knowledge warrants respect and sensitivity. Recently, various communities throughout the world have turned to intellectual property laws to preserve, protect and promote their traditional knowledge. Certain communities have also sought to make equitable use of their traditional knowledge. Currently, only a few nations offer explicit *sui generie* protection for traditional knowledge. Faced with exploitation of Indian traditional knowledge by few developed nations, India has started addressing the issue through various measures, including establishing a mechanism namely Traditional Knowledge Digital Library (TKDL), essentially to protect such information from being furiously exploited and also to foster socio-economic development of the communities that made the knowledge survive for long. The TKDL is a searchable database and is being made accessible globally thwarting patenting of such traditional knowledge by unscrupulous elements.

Domain Name

The term domain name has multiple meanings that are related to the:

- The product that registrars provide to their customers,
- Name that is entered into a computer (e.g. as part of a Web site or other URL, or an e-mail address) and then looked up in the global domain Name System, which informs the computer of the IP addresses with the name.
- A name looked up in the DNS for other purposes.

They are sometimes colloquially (and incorrectly) referred to "Web addresses" by marketers. The authoritative definition is that "domain names are hostnames that provide more easily memorable names to stand in for numeric IP addresses". They allow for any service to move to a different location in the topology of the Internet, which would then have a different IP address.

Exclusive Rights

The rights conferred by intellectual property rights are described as exclusive rights. The exclusive rights granted by intellectual property laws are generally negative in nature, and therefore only grant the holder of IP the ability to exclude third parties from infringing on their monopoly. The exclusive rights conferred by intellectual property laws can generally be transferred, licensed or mortgaged to third parties. It may also be possible to use intellectual property as security for a loan. Exclusive rights are divided into two categories viz., those that grant exclusive rights only on copying and those that grant a right to prevent others from doing same thing. Thus, exclusive rights ban unauthorized reproduction and commercial exploitation. Economic theory suggests that a free market with no exclusive rights will lead to too little production of intellectual works relative to an efficient outcome. Thus, by increasing rewards for authors, inventors and other producers of intellectual works overall efficiency might be improved.

One argument against IPR is that laws are so stringent that they hurt the public interest more than they help. Another argument is that the term operates as a catch- all to lump together desperate laws originated separately, evolved differently, cover different activities, have different rules, and raise different public policy issues. So it is better to discuss and refer various laws individually.

Conclusion

In recent times there has been a general expansion in intellectual property laws. This can be seen in the extension of laws to new types of subject matter such as databases, in the regulation of new categories of activity, in respect of subject matter already protected, in the increase of terms of protection, in the removal of restrictions and limitation on exclusive rights. Though the subject matter is different, they all share a common trait in granting the 'owner' of the exclusive rights a monopoly on the copying or distribution of a protected form of property. Nevertheless, it has an unintended consequence, namely treating abstract rules and mental products like concert leading to stifling of innovation in those fields, rather than aiding. The nature and scope of what constitutes intellectual property has also expanded. The grant of patents in some jurisdictions covering certain life forms, software algorithms, and business models has led to ongoing controversy over the appropriate scope of patentable subject matter. Expansion of intellectual property laws upsets the balance between encouraging and facilitating creativity and innovation and the dissemination of new ideas and creations into the public domain for the common good. Innovation and competition is in effect stifled by expanding IP laws, as litigious IP rights holders aggressively or frivolously seek to protect their portfolios. In a sense, such litigious milieu is also a good thing to happen to the human community, as the famous philosopher

J.Krishnamoorthy (JK), has commented, "Where there is conflict, there will be a solution to it".

References

Das, B.B., 2005 Enforcement of right of author under copyright law: AIR Jour. 74.

Information Technology Act and Applicability of IPR with Special reference to law of copyrights (2002) 1 SCJ.

Khehra, H.K., 2004 Registration of plant varieties in India: Life and effect of Protection: AIR.Jour.281.

Misra, D.N., 2004 International investment law, W.T.O and Intellectual Property rights with special reference to W.T.O.: DSV in developing countries: Indian Bar Review. V.XXX1.

Mukherjee, D.C., 1988 Some common problems of world trademarks laws and prescriptions: AIR.Jour.151.

Patel, J., 2002 Copyright enforcement in India and global world:. Comment on copyright: RF whale. AIR Jour.209.

Sangal, P.S. 1999 Trade marks and domain names: Some recent developments: JILI v. 41.

Sharma, S.D., 2005 Human skill creation under copyright as an exclusive human right. AIR Jour.11.

Singh, S.K., 2002 Trade related intellectual property rights (TRIPS) Agreement and Indian legal system! Some suggestions. AIR. Jour.216.

Trade Marks, Industrial Designs and Copyrights (2002) 4 SCJ.

Intellectual Property Rights Demystified, 2008
Mu. Ramkumar & A. Jayakumar (ed.), pp. 25-39
New India Publishing Agency, New Delhi (India)
E-mail : newindiapublishingagency@gmail.com
Web: www.bookfactoryindia.com

3

Review on Recent Developments in Registration of Inventions and Protection of IPR in India

***T.POONGODI VIJAYAKUMAR AND **Mu.RAMKUMAR**
*Department of Food Science, **Department of Geology, Periyar University, Salem - 636 011.

ABSTRACT

This paper provides an overview on existing IP protection and registration systems of India and adds information culled from publicly available sources pertaining to modernization efforts of Government of India towards establishment of foolproof IP protection in accordance with international treaties, conventions and bilateral and multilateral agreements.

INTRODUCTION

Intellectual Property is the name commonly given to a group of separate intangible properties viz., trademarks, patents, copyrights, designs, plant varieties and the layout designs of integrated circuits. As most of the IP rights granted by Nation States are territorial, prohibition of infringement in other territories becomes complex and costlier. The efforts of writers, artists, designers and inventors need to be protected to create an environment where creativity can flourish and hard work can be rewarded. This paper presents information on how effectively the creative works are being protected through existing legal milieu in India.

INTELLECTUAL PROPERTY

Following the emergence of strong global and national intellectual property regimes, protection of IPR has become a central issue in economic development, scientific and technological development, protection of traditional knowledge and scientific and economic cooperation between industrialized and developing countries. There is a strong opposition or apprehension particularly in developing countries to the very idea of the necessity of strong intellectual property regimes. It is believed that only the developed countries will profit from it. Nevertheless, it is also advocated by a section of the society that 'establishing ownership of intellectual assets and arriving at acceptable frameworks for fair and equitable sharing of benefits for social good and providing harmonized legal structures to encourage continuous flow of innovation are bare necessities to fuel a vibrant global economy. The convention establishing the World Intellectual Property Organization (WIPO) concluded in Stockholm on July 14, 1967 (Article 2) (viii) provides that "Intellectual property" shall include rights relating to:

- Literary, artistic and scientific works,
- Performances of performing artists, phonograms and broadcasts,
- Inventions in all fields of human endeavor,
- Scientific discoveries,
- Industrial designs,
- Trademarks, service marks, and commercial names and designs.
- Protection against unfair competition and all other rights resulting from intellectual activity in the industrial, scientific, literacy or artistic fields.

REQUISITES FOR REGISTRATION OF INVENTIONS

An invention may be defined as an idea of making a new and useful article, method or substance. The WIPO Model Law for Developing Countries on Inventions (1979) defines invention 'as an idea of an inventor, which permits in practice the solution of a specific problem in a field of technology.' The term 'invention' comes from the Latin word *'invenire'*, which means 'to come upon'. With most inventions, there is a sense of surprise. There may be many reasons for making inventions. The important are:

- For personal satisfaction and to make money,
- For solving a problem faced in everyday life,
- For being recognized by others and
- For the desire to take up a challenging/interesting task.

Not all inventions are patentable. The basic criteria for an invention to be patentable as required by the patent laws of almost all the countries are:

- It must be novel.
- It must involve an inventive step or it must be non-obvious and
- It must have some industrial application.

However, even if the invention is new, it may not be patentable according to the patent laws of certain countries. Similarly, certain articles, processes or ideas cannot be protected even if they are new. Things that are non-patentable in India (Ganguli 1988) are listed herein.

- Frivolous claims contrary to well-established natural laws.
- Anything contrary to law or morality, or injurious to public health.
- Mere arrangement or rearrangement or duplication of known devices, each functioning independently of one another in a known way.
- A method or process of testing applicable during the process of manufacture for rendering the machine, apparatus or other

equipment more efficient or for the improvement or restoration of the existing machine, apparatus or other equipment or for the improvement or control of manufacture.

- A method of agriculture or horticulture.
- Inventions related to atomic energy.
- Computer software.
- Aesthetic creations.
- Discoveries, scientific theories, mathematical methods.
- Schemes, rules or methods for performing mental acts, playing games or doing business, presentation of information.
- Methods of treating humans or animals through surgery, or therapeutics and diagnostics.
- Animals and plants and biological methods for rearing/growing them (however, microorganism is patentable in India).
- Products made by chemical synthesis of foods and medicines.

For every invention, there should be a separate patent application. However, if a group of inventions are so-linked to form a single general inventive concept, one application will suffice. In India, a patent application must be drafted in english. A patent application should include the following:

- The object or title of the invention.
- Prior art or cross-references to related applications, if any.
- Brief summary of the invention.
- Brief description of several views of the drawing, if need be.
- Detailed description of the invention.
- Claim or claims and
- An abstract of the disclosure.

While the Controller General of Patents, Designs and Trademarks (CGPDTM) functioning under the aegis of the Department of Industrial Development controls patents, designs and trademarks, the Ministry of Human Resources is the custodian of copyright protection.

PROTECTION OF INTELLECTUAL PROPERTY IN INDIA

The importance of intellectual property in India is well entrenched through statutory, administrative and judicial levels. India ratified the agreement establishing the World Trade Organization (WTO). This Agreement, inter-alias, contains an Agreement on Trade Related Aspects of Intellectual Property Rights (TRIPS), which came into force from 1st January 1995. It lays down minimum standards for protection and enforcement of intellectual property rights in member countries, which required to promote effective and adequate protection of intellectual property rights with a view to reducing distortions and impediments to international trade. The obligations under the TRIPS Agreement relate to provision of minimum standard of protection within the member countrie's legal systems and practices.

As a signatory to the TRIPS Agreement, India required to align its laws on intellectual property rights in accordance with the obligations. Legislations are being made in conformity to obligations under the TRIPS Agreement, relating to 'Patents, Trademarks. Geographical Indications and Industrial Designs have been amended/ enacted. As on date, these legislations are fully in compliance with its TRIPS obligations. While making the existing legal provisions with these obligations, many revamps, modernizations and simplifications of procedures were also taken up by India.

The office of the Controller General of Patents, Designs and Trade Marks (CGPDTM) administers the working of the Patents Act, 1970, the Designs Act, 2000 and the Trade and Merchandise Marks Act, 1958 and renders advice to the Government on matters relating to industrial property rights. In addition, functioning of the Patent Office (including Designs Wing), Patent Information System

(PIS), the Trade Marks Registry (TMR) and the Geographical Indications Registry (GIR) are being managed by this office.

Patents

The TRIPS Agreement provides for a minimum term of protection of 20 years counted from the date of filing. India had already implemented its obligations under Articles 70.8 and 70.9 of TRIPS Agreement. A comprehensive review of the Patents Act, 1970 was also made and a bill to amend the Patents Act, 1970 was passed by Parliament. The amendment to the Patent Law has been made operational from 20.05.2003.

The Patent Office performs its statutory duties in connection with the grant of patents for new inventions under the Patents Act, 1970 modified by the Patents (Amendment) Act, 1999 and registration of industrial designs under the Designs Act, 2000. The Head Office is at Kolkatta with branches at Mumbai, Chennai and Delhi. The branches deal with the applications for patents originating within their respective territorial jurisdiction. The Patents (Amendment) Act, 1999 provides for filing of product patent applications related to pharmaceutical and agro-chemicals and grant of Exclusive Marketing Right (EMR) on these applications.

Patent Information system (PIS) at Nagpur has been functioning as patent information base for the users since 1980. The PIS maintains a comprehensive collection of patent specification and patent related literature, on a world-wide basis and provides technological information contained in patent or patent related literature. This system offers thorough search services and patent copy supply services to various users of R & D establishments, government offices, private industries, business houses inventors and other users within India.

Industrial Designs

The duration of protection for Industrial designs is to be not less than 10 years. A new designs law repealing and replacing the Designs Act, 1911 has been passed by Parliament in the Budget Session, 2000. This Act has been brought into force from

11.5.2001. The registration of industrial designs under the Designs Act, 2000 is done by the Designs Wing of the Head Office of Patents located at Kolkata. The Designs Act, 2000 provides a wider ambit of coverage and incorporates newer features that harmonized the Indian legal system with laws of other countries.

Trademarks

Trademarks have been defined as any sign, or any combination of signs capable of distinguishing the goods or services of one undertaking from those of other undertakings. Such distinguishing marks constitute protectable subject matter under the provisions of the TRIPS Agreement. The Agreement provides that initial registration and each renewal of registration shall be for a term of not less than 7 years and the registration shall be renewable indefinitely. Compulsory licensing of trademarks is not permitted. Keeping in view the changes in trade and commercial practices, globalization of trade, need for simplification and harmonization of trade marks registration systems etc., a comprehensive review of the Trade and Merchandise Marks Act, 1958 was made and a Bill to repeal and replace the 1958 Act has since been passed by Parliament and notified in the Gazette on 30.12.1999. This Act not only made the Trade Marks Law to be TRIPS compatibile but also harmonizes it with international systems and practices. The subordinate legislation of the laws on Trade Marks has also been modified.

The Trade Marks Registry (TMR) administers the Trade and Merchandise Marks Act, 1958. The TMR receives and processes applications for the registration, renewal or cancellation of trademarks and other related functions. It also undertakes activities for information dissemination and awareness generation. With India becoming signatory to many international treaties and conventions, the Registry had embarked on a major drive to modernize the system and functions. As a result of which, online registration of trademark applications in all the regional offices and head quarter has begun from October 2002. Digital database library on CD-ROMs of 1,50,000 Trade Mark Certificates and 1,250 Trade Marks Journals has also been created and made available for reference.

Geographical Indications

A new law for the protection of geographical indications, viz. the Geographical Indications of Goods (Registration and the Protection) Act, 1999 has also been passed by the Parliament and notified on 30.12.1999. The subordinate legislation of the laws on Geographical Indications has been modified.

Under the Geographical Indications of goods (Registration and Protection) Act, 1999, a Geographical Indications Registry was operationalized in Chennai in August 2001. The Registry is a modern office, which integrates IT enabled processes in its operations. The Registry has commenced creating awareness on GI through conductance of seminars in cooperation with local chambers of commerce and State and Central governments. The registry also provides guidance to potential applicants with regard to the protection of names of goods, which originate in a specific and identifiable geographical territory within the country in order to safeguard the intellectual property inherent in such indications of source.

Copyrights

India's copyright law, laid down in the Indian Copyright Act, 1957 as amended by Copyright (Amendment) Act, 1999, fully reflects the Berne Convention on Copyrights, to which India is a party. Additionally, India is party to the Geneva Convention for the Protection of rights of Producers of Phonograms and to the Universal Copyright Convention. India is also an active member of the World Intellectual Property Organization (WIPO), Geneva and UNESCO. The copyright law has been amended periodically to keep pace with changing requirements. The recent amendment to the copyright law, which came into force in May 1995, has ushered in comprehensive changes and brought the copyright law in line with the developments in satellite broadcasting, computer software and digital technology. The amended law has made provisions for the first time, to protect performer's rights as envisaged in the Rome Convention. Several other measures have been adopted to strengthen and streamline the enforcement of copyrights. These include setting up of a Copyright Enforcement Advisory Council, training programs for enforcement officers and setting up special policy cells to deal with cases relating to infringement of copyrights.

MODERNIZATION INITIATIVES OF INDIA

In order to be in tune with the obligations of many international conventions and treaties, the Indian government has taken up comprehensive modernization of intellectual property administration as detailed herein. These are collated from publicly available information as disseminated by governmental agencies.

- The infrastructure for Patent Offices in Delhi, Kolkata, Chennai and Mumbai have been fully modernized and operationalized.
- A completely modernized and computerized Designs Office in Kolkata has been made operational.
- Action is underway to set up Integrated IP Offices in each of the four metro cities so as to house all activities in one building.
- A logo for IP administration has been designed and put into use.
- A website (http://www.ipindia.nic.in) of IP offices has been launched. This is being redesigned to make it user-friendlier.
- Computerized information System for intimating status of patent applications is established. Comprehensive computerization is underway.
- Online search facilities have been established and were linked with international databases.
- 227 posts of Examiners of Patents have been created and most of the vacancies are filled.
- An Intellectual Property Training Institute (IPTI) has been established at Nagpur to provide training to newly recruited Examiners and others engaged in the field of intellectual property rights.
- Work manuals for IP offices have been prepared to ensure uniformity in their operation.

- Digital database of over 1,00,000 patent records and 48,000 design records has been prepared so far. A searchable database will be put on the website.
- Online linkage of all branch offices from 1st October 2002 had allowed the branches to receive applications and issue allocation numbers through online on the very day of receipt of application.
- Creation of physical files and data entry are being done by the end of the next working day. Earlier, it took up to 9 months.
- Examination of applications is being done within a week of receipt of application. Earlier, it took upto 5 years.
- With the consolidation of work and induction of new Examiners, the overall performance had improved further. Now it is possible to ensure grant of patent rights within a timeframe comparable to international levels and consistent with the statutory provisions.
- The problem of backlog of pending patent applications has also been addressed through legislative measures contained in the Patents (Amendment) Act, 2002 which introduced examination on request system in place of examination of all applications.
- Publication in TM Journal is being done within 15 days while it took 6 months earlier.
- Renewal of TM Certificates is being done in Clear Cases on the very day of application. In other Cases, renewal is being done within 2 months. Earlier it took more than a year.
- All functions up to clarification stages are decentralized. Earlier all activities were centralized at the Headquarter, Mumbai.

Conclusion

Although Indian society has practiced universality of knowledge and adhered to the principle of making common good with the immeasurable knowledge it possessed since time immemorial, current scenario of drawing economic incentive from knowledge had made India to strive hard to become chief knowledge supplier in many frontiers of scientific endeavors for the benefit of humankind in general, socio-economic welfare of Indians in particular. This change in mindset of Indian society is being brought in since the signing up of many international treaties and conventions that obligated India to establish legal and administrative systems in compliance with the provisions contained in the accords. However, long and grueling journey is ahead as in spite of all these efforts, there still is a disparity among number of patent applications and patents granted as per the statistics available with patent office of India (Janodia *et al.* 2007).

References

Ganguli, P., 1998 Gearing up for patents: The Indian Scenario. Universities Press (India) Ltd.

Janodia, M.D., Sreedhar, D., Ligade, V.S., Pise, A.G. and Udupa, N., 2007 Patent office and patent applications – Bridging the disparity. Curr.Sci. v.93. pp.124.

APPENDIX – I

List of international and regional agreements/treaties of IPR

(1886) Berne convention for the Protection of Literacy and Artistic Works.

(1891) Madrid Agreement for the Repression of False or Deceptive Indications of Source of Goods.

(1891) Madrid Agreement Concerning the International Registration of Marks.

(1925) Hague Agreement concerning the International Deposit of Industrial Designs.

(1957) Nice Agreement concerning the International Classification of Goods and Services for the Purpose of the Registration of Marks.

(1958) Lisbon Agreement for the Protection of Appellations of Origin and their International Registration.

(1961) Rome Convention for the Protection of Performers, Producers of Phonograms and Broadcasting Organizations.

(1968) Locarno Agreement Establishing an International Classification for Industrial Design.

(1970) Patent convention Treaty ("PCT").

(1971) Strasbourg Agreement Concerning the International Patent Classification.

(1971) Geneva Convention for the Protection of Producers of Phonograms Against Unauthorized Duplication of Their Phonograms.

(1973) Vienna Agreement Establishing an International Classification of the Figurative Elements of Marks.

(1974) Brussels Convention Relating to the Distribution of Programme-Carrying Signals Transmitted by Satellite.

(1977) Budapest Treaty on the International Recognition of the Deposit of Microorganisms for the purpose of Patent procedure.

(1981) Nairobi Treaty on the Protection of the Olympic Symbol.

(1989) Washington Treaty on Intellectual Property in Respect of Integrated Circuits.

(1989) Protocol Relating to the Madrid Agreement Concerning the International Registration.

(1994) Trademark Law Treaty ("TLT") (1994).

(1994) Trade Related Intellectual Property Rights ("TRIPS").

(1996) Community Trademarks (1996).

(1996) Documents of the Diplomatic Conference on Certain Copyright and Neighboring Rights Questions (Geneva, December 2-20).

(1996) WIPO Copyright Treaty (WCT).

(1996) WIPO Performance and Phonograms Treaty (WPPT).

APPENDIX – II

Basic Information on requirements for claiming IPR

a.	Competent receiving office	The Patent Office, Kolkata, and its branch Offices at New Delhi, Mumbai, Chennai (RO/IN) International Bureau (RO/IB), Geneva, Switzerland.
b.	Language of filing	RO/IN : English, Hindi RO/IB : Any language
c.	Elements of the International application	i. Request (PCT/RO/101) ii. Description iii. One or more claims iv. Abstract v. Drawings (where applicable) vi. Fees vii P.A./G.P.A. (where applicable)
d.	No. of copies required	RO/IN : 3 (i to v) to The Patent Office, Kolkata and 4 (i to v above) to the above Patent Office Branch, New Delhi, Mumbai, Chennai RO/IB : 1
e.	Competent International Searching Authorities [ISAs]	Austrian Patent Office (AT) Australian Patent Office (AU) European Patent Office (EP) China Intellectual Property Office (CN) United States Patent & Trademark Office (US) Swedish Patent Office (SE)
f.	Competent International Preliminary Examining Authorities [IPEAs]	Austrian Patent Office (AT) Australian Patent Office (AU) European Patent Office (EP) China Intellectual Property Office (CN) United States Patent & Trademark Office (US) Swedish Patent Office (SE)

APPENDIX – III

Number of patents filed in various countries

Country	Number of patents filed (Residents)	Number of patents filed (Non-residents)
USA	127476	107964
CHINA	10066	31707
BRAZIL	2757	23040
SRILANKA	76	15944
MALAYSIA	141	39113
PAKISTAN	21	678
INDIA	1545	5021

Intellectual Property Rights Demystified, 2008
Mu. Ramkumar & A. Jayakumar (ed.), pp. 41-44
New India Publishing Agency, New Delhi (India)
E-mail : newindiapublishingagency@gmail.com
Web: www.bookfactoryindia.com

4

An Introduction to Patenting System of India

V. A. AMBIGAPATHY
Patent Office, Chennai.

ABSTRACT

This paper presents an outline on the patenting system prevailing in India.

INTRODUCTION

Ideas and knowledge are increasingly important parts of trade. Most of the value of new medicines and other high technology products lies in the amount of invention, innovation, research, design and testing involved. Hence, protection of such values is paramount. This paper details how these values are protected in India.

INTELLECTUAL PROPERTY RIGHTS

Intellectual Property Rights (IPR) play an important role in the international trade and commerce and also in the industrial, economical and social development of a nation. Patents, Designs, Trademarks, Geographical Indications, Copyright and similar rights are referred to as "intellectual property".

Patents protect inventions such as machines, devices, methods and compositions of matter. Trademark rights protect words, designs, numbers, 2-d or 3-d forms (or a combination of two or more of these elements) used to distinguish the products or services of one trader from those of others in the market place. Geographical indication protects a given product originating in a specific geographical area. The underlying idea is that certain products owe their special qualities to the place from which they come e.g., Basmati rice, Nagpur oranges, Darjeeling tea etc. Copyright protects literary (including computer program), artistic, musical and dramatic works. Related rights include trade secrets, industrial designs, integrated circuit topographies, plant breeder's rights and personality rights such as the right to the image. Trademark protection can be maintained indefinitely. Patent, copyright and industrial design enjoy protection only for limited time that can be renewed.

India has been a signatory to many international agreements, which have evolved for regulating grant and exploitation of IPR. As a result, IPR related activities have been on continuous increase in our country for the last several years. Many complex issues are involved in creation, utilization and meaningful exploitation of IPR. The laws governing intellectual property rights are necessarily techno-legal matters.

PATENTING SYSTEM

Patent means *'to be open'* i.e., open to public inspection. The fundamental principle of patent law is that any subject matter to be patentable must be an invention and not a discovery. There is always a difference between discovery and invention. The discovery adds to the amount of human knowledge by disclosing something, which has not been seen before, whereas an invention also adds to the human knowledge by suggesting an act, to be done which results in a new product or a new process.

According to Sec 2(1)(j) of The Patents Act, 1970 "invention" means a new product or process involving an inventive step and capable of industrial application. The patentable subject matter should relate to a manner of manufacture, which includes not only a process of manufacture but also a manufactured product.

The first step in securing a patent is the filing of a patent application in Patent office. The patent application generally contains the title of the invention, as well as the indication of its technical field; it must include the background and a description of the invention in clear language with enough details so that an individual with an average understanding of the field could use or reproduce the invention. Visual materials such as drawings or diagrams to better describe the invention usually accompany such descriptions. The application ends with "claims", *(backbone of the patent specification)*, which determines the extent of protection granted by the patent. The claims define the essential characteristics of the invention. The application must accompany an abstract pertaining to a brief technical subject of the invention.

Economics drive the filing of patent applications. The philosophy behind the grant of patent is *"suffer less evil for more good"* and the purpose is to stimulate the investment in industrial innovation.

Once obtained, the patent is a property, which can be sold (assigned) or licensed, or the first patent owner may bring the invention protected by the patent to the market place. If a patent is licensed (assigned), the patent still is the property of the patent owner but the licensee can use the invention under conditions set out in a license agreement.

The patent right is territorial in nature and inventors/their assignees will have to file separate applications in countries of their interest, for obtaining patents in those countries.

Conclusion

Patents enrich the total body of technical knowledge by publicly disclosing the information. Such an ever-increasing body of public knowledge promotes further creativity and innovation in others. In this way, patents provide not only protection for the owner but valuable information and inspiration for future generations of researchers and inventors.

The extent of protection and enforcement of these rights varied widely around the world. As intellectual property became more important in trade, these differences became a source of tension in international economic relations. New international trade rules for intellectual property rights were seen as a way to introduce more order and predictability and for disputes to be settled more systematically.

Few of the common application forms for registering designs, patents, trademarks, etc., are provided at the end of this volume as annexure for the use of readers. However, before submission of filled-in forms, readers are requested to consult the nearest patent office for any recent version and the amount of fee to be remitted. In addition to these forms, there are various other forms for filing objection, extension of protection time, renewal of copyright, modification of any information contained in previous application, etc., and those who are in need of these forms, may contact the nearest Patent office.

References

The Patents Act, 1970

http://Patentoffice.nic.in

http://ipindia.nic.in

www.wipo.int

www.wto.org

Intellectual Property Rights Demystified, 2008
Mu. Ramkumar & A. Jayakumar (ed.), pp. 45-54
New India Publishing Agency, New Delhi (India)
E-mail : newindiapublishingagency@gmail.com
Web: www.bookfactoryindia.com

5

Copyright Laws of India: An Introduction

***V.THILLAIKUMAR AND +S. GAYATHRI**
*District Court, Namakkal. +M. Kumarasamy College of Engineering, Karur.

ABSTRACT

Intellectual property right (IPR) is the most serious, new branch of law and a legal right conferred by federal government in accordance with International conventions and treaties. IPR protects some of the finer manifestations of human achievement. IPR safeguards the application of ideas and information that are of commercial value. The exploitable ideas become more sophisticated and hope for a successful economic future depends increasingly upon the superior corpus of new knowledge and fashionable conceits. Copyright law is one of the effective tools of IPR. Copyright law provides an incentive to creative activity of author and permits the society to benefit from those inventions. However, the technological advancement has made violation of copyright very easy and regulation very difficult. This paper aims at familiarizing copyright laws and the powers enshrined in copyright laws.

INTRODUCTION

Copyright is a protection that covers published and unpublished literary, scientific and artistic works, whatever be the form of expression, provided such works are fixed in a tangible or material form. The importance of copyright as Intellectual property has increased enormously in recent times, due to rapid technological development in the fields of printing, communication, entertainment and computers. Hence there is a need for the authors to derive economic benefits from their own creative work while serving the cause of developments in science and society.

COPYRIGHT – AN EXTENSION OF RIGHT TO EXPRESSION

Almost all democratic constitutions provide a guarantee for right to freedom of speech and expression. The laws of copyright enhance the value of such freedom through effective protection to the creative works, from being reproduced without a licence. If an individual has freedom of speech and expression, then he/she will get a right to protect an intellectual work as property.

Indian Copyright Act, 1957

The copyright Act 1957 and the copyright rules 1958 with relevant amendment, is the law applicable in India. The underlying principle of copyright protection is that specific, creative expressions are protected but not the ideas behind them. Copyright comes into existence as soon as a work is created.

Term of Protection

Original literary, dramatic, musical and artistic works enjoy copyright protection for the lifetime of the author plus 60 years. The term of protection is 60 years since publication in the case of cinematography films, records, posthumous, anonymous and pseudonymous publications.

Economic Rights of Copyright Owners

Copyright owners generally have the right to authorize or prohibit any and all of the following pertaining to their work.

- Copying the work in anyway.
- Issuing copies of the work to the public.

- Renting or lending copies of the work to the public.
- Performing, showing or playing the work in public.
- Broadcasting the work or other communication to the public by electronic transmission and Making an adaptation of the work.

Copyright is infringed when any of the above are done without authorization, whether directly or indirectly.

Infringement of Copyright

Infringement of copyright refers to the reproduction of a literary, dramatic, musical or artistic work without a license granted by the owner of copyright or the Registrar of copyright. Anybody who uses, copies or distributes copyrighted material for commercial or personal purpose, without the author's permission, would be committing an infringement of copyright. Here, Ignorance of Law does not make one exempt from compliance thereof.

Intention is Irrelevant

Once the copyright is infringed, the motive or intention of violation is irrelevant. If the conditions under section 51 are satisfied and none of the exceptions specified in section 52 are applicable, the infringement would invite the penalty prescribed under the law, irrespective of the good, naive or lofty intention of the violator.

Fair use

A copyright work can be used without the consent of the copyright holder to facilitate education, research, dissemination of knowledge and information, for promotion of economy and culture of a society. The doctrine of fair use permits the copying of protected work for reasonable purpose without profit motive. In the case of fair use, it is essential that one must credit the author's hard work by naming the source as a reference.

REGISTRATION OF COPYRIGHT

- Every application for registration of copyright shall be made in accordance with form IV (*provided at the end of this paper*).
- Every application shall be in respect of one work only, shall be made in triplicate, accompanied by the prescribed fee.
- The person applying for registration shall give notice of his/ her application to every person who claims or has any interest in the subject matter of the copyright.
- If no such objection is received by the Registrar of copyright within thirty days of the receipt of the application, he/she shall, if satisfied about the correctness of the particulars given in the application, enter it in the Register of copyright.
- If the Registrar of copyright receives any objection for such registration within the time specified, he/she may, after holding such inquiry as he deems fit, enter such particular in the Register.

Act of Piracy and Burden of Proof

The violation of copyright amounts to an act of piracy. It must be proved by clear and cogent evidence, after applying the relevant texts and conditions prescribed by the copyright law and the burden is on the person who alleges the violation of his/her copyright. The originality of work and fact of violation has to be established by him/her. Then the burden shifts on the defendant to show that he/she had a fair dealing or that he/she would be within the framework of exception.

Remedies

Infringement of copyright is a cognizable and non bailable offence, which is punishable with imprisonment from 6 months up to 3 years and with fine from Rs. 50,000/- to Rs.2,00,000/- (Section 63). Subsequent infringements call for enhanced punishment of minimum imprisonment of one year and minimum fine of Rs. 1,00,000/- (Sec 63A). Sub Inspectors and Senior Police officers have been given powers to seize the infringing copies and all plates used for making them without warrants. Owner of copyright is entitled to seek civil remedies by injunction, damages, accounts and otherwise (Section 55).

Right to Transfer or Assign Copyright

According to the Act, copyright can be transferred to another, like any other property. It may be bequeathed by will, gifted or sold. Such a disposal of copyright is called 'Assignment'. An assignment may be for reproduction in one form only and in one country only.

Copyrights and The Internet

Material found on the web may be copied freely only if the information is created by the Federal Government or the term of Copyright has been expired or abandoned by the holder. Any work published on the internet is not automatically placed in the public domain, unless the material in question complied with one or more or the characteristics mentioned.

Conclusion

"Where the mind is without fears and the head is held high;
Where knowledge is free; Into the heaven of freedom, my father,
let my country awake".

From these words of Rabindranath Tagore, we come to know that our culture believes in dissemination of knowledge. In a modern knowledge society of the democratic world, the research is a continuing process and everyone, in any corner of the world must have freedom to develop from earlier thought and safeguard the work for the most innovative usage. However, there is still a need to protect the copyright of the authors from clever publishers and commercial exploiters. There is a strong need for the authors, creative artists and research scientists to come together and form associations like copyright societies to make use of the powers provided in the copyright. A balanced approach is needed for facilitating free flow of knowledge and protecting the interests of creative artists.

Acknowledgements

We are thankful to the organizers of the workshop GEO-IPR'2006 for providing exposure to the most innovative concepts. The reviewers and editors are thanked for having helped us to rephrase the earlier version of the manuscript to its present form.

References

Madabhushi Sridhar, 2002 The Right Regime of copyright, ICFAI Journal of Intellectual Property Rights.

Intellectual Property Law in India – Justice P. S. Narayana.

Contd...

FORM IV
Application for Registration of Copyright

To
The Registrar of Copyrights,
Copyright Office, New Delhi.

Sir,

In accordance with section 45 of the Copyright Act, 1957 (14 of 1957), I hereby apply for registration of copyright and request that entries may be made in the Register of Copyrights as in the enclosed Statement of Particulars sent herewith in triplicate.

1. [1][also send herewith duly completed the Statement of further particulars relating to the work.
2. In accordance with rule 16 of the Copyright Rules, 1958, I have sent by prepaid registered post copies of this letter and of the enclosed statement(s) to the other parties[2] concerned, as shown below:

Name and addresses	Date of dispatch of the parties

The prescribed fee has been paid, as per details below:

3. Communications of this subject may be addressed to.
4. [3][I hereby declare that to the best of my knowledge and belief, no person, other than to whom a notice has been sent as per paragraph 2 above any claim or interest or dispute to my copyright of this work or to its use by me].

Place :
Date :

Yours faithfully
(Signature)

1. For Literary, Dramatic, Musical and Artistic works only.
2. See columns 7, 11, 12 and 13 of the Statement of Particulars and the party referred to in column 2(e) of the Statement of Further Particulars.
3. Inserted by Notification No. GSR 435(E), dated 17–4–1992, w.e.f. 17-4-1992.
4. Renumbered by Notification No. GSR 435(E), dated 27–4-1992, w.e.f. 27-4-1992.

STATEMENT OF PARTICULARS (To be sent in triplicate)

1. Registration Number. (To be filled in the Copyright Office)
2. Name, address and nationality of the applicant.
3. Nature of the applicant's interest in the copyright of the work.
4. Class and description of the work.
5. Title of the work.
6. Language of the work.
7. Name, address and nationality of the author and if the author is deceased, the date of his/her decease.
8. Whether work is published or unpublished.
9. Year and country of first publication and name, address and nationality of the publisher.
10. Years and countries of subsequent publications, if any, and names, addresses and nationalities of the publishers.
11. Names, address and nationalities of the owners of the various rights comprising the copyright in the work and the extent of rights held by each, together with particulars of assignments and licenses, if any.
12. Names, addresses and nationalities of other persons, if any, authorized to assign or license the rights comprising the copyright.

13. If the work is an "Artistic Work", the location of the Original work, including name, address and nationality of the person in possession of the work. (In the case of an architectural work, the year of completion of the work should also be shown).

13A. If the work is an "artistic work" which is used or is capable of being used in relation to any goods, the application shall include a certificate from the Registration of Trade Marks in terms of the proviso to sub-section (1) of section 45 of the Copyright Act, 1957].

14. Remarks, if any.

Place :

Date : (*Signature*)

Statement of Further Particulars

(To be sent in triplicate)

[For Literary, Dramatic, Musical and Artistic Works only]

1. Is the work to be registered:
   (a) an original work ?
   (b) a translation of work in the public domain?
   (c) A translation of a work in which copyright subsists?

2. For Literary, Dramatic, Musical and Artistic works only.
   (a) an adaptation of a work in the public domain?
   (b) An adaptation of work in which copyright subsists?

3. If the work is a translation or adaptation of work in which copyright subsists:
   (a) Title of the original work
   (b) Language of the original work.
   (c) Name, address, and nationality of the author of the original work and if the author is deceased, the date of decease.
   (d) Name, address and nationality of the publisher, if any, of the original work.
   (e) Particulars of the authorization for a translation or adaptation including the name, address and nationality of the party authorizing.

Place :

Date : *(Signature)*

Intellectual Property Rights Demystified, 2008
Mu. Ramkumar & A. Jayakumar (ed.), pp. 55-62
New India Publishing Agency, New Delhi (India)
E-mail : newindiapublishingagency@gmail.com
Web: www.bookfactoryindia.com

6

World Intellectual Property Organization (WIPO) and Its Role in Promotion and Protection of IPR

M.A. THAMIZH SELVI
Central Law College, Salem.

ABSTRACT

This paper provides an overall view on the history, structure and functions of World Intellectual Property Rights Organization.

INTRODUCTION

"*Human genius is the source of all works of art and invention. These works are the guarantees of a life worthy of men. It is duty of the state to ensure with diligence the protection of the arts and inventions,*" reads an inscription on the copula in the WIPO Headquarters building in Geneva. True to this inscription, WIPO functions through various mechanisms fostering judicious utilization of human intellect. This paper intends presenting an overview on WIPO.

The World Intellectual Property Organization (WIPO) is an international organization dedicated to promoting the use and protection of works of the human spirit. These works – intellectual property – are expanding the bounds of science and technology and enriching the world of the arts. Through its work, WIPO plays an important role in enhancing the quality and enjoyment of life, as well as creating real wealth for nations.

With headquarters in Geneva, Switzerland, WIPO is one of the 16 specialized agencies of the United Nations system of organizations. It administers 23 international treaties dealing with different aspects of intellectual property protection. The Organization counts 183 nations as member states.

WHY INTELLECTUAL PROPERTY IS TO BE PROTECTED?

Any property, movable or immovable is to be legally protected in order to prevent misappropriation/misuse. Similarly, intellectual property needs also to be protected from infringement. In modern times, the term "IP" is being used to include all properties resulting from the application of human intellect. World over, the IPR laws resulted by the GATT agreement and the establishment of WTO and WIPO.

Only knowledge that is protected can have the potential of wealth creation. IPR's are the exclusive rights granted by the state as a reward for the disclosure of the inventions resulting from creative and innovative activities. The WIPO is the UN's specialized agency for inter-governmental co-operation in "Industrial Property" and "copyright and neighboring rights". WIPO carries out a substantial programme of activities in the field of IP to promote creative intellectual activity, protection of IP, International co-operation and the transfer of technology, especially to and among developing countries.

Protection of the invention is the object of the law of IPR and such protection encourages research and development. With the development of society, new discoveries and inventions are made, thus widening the items that fall under the category of intellectual property. IP law protects the results of human creative endeavor. IP comprises four separate broad fields of law, namely Trademarks, copyrights, patents and trade secrets. A trademark is a word, name, symbol, or device used to indicate the origin, quality and ownership of a product or service. Copyright protects original works of authorship, including literary, musical, dramatic, artistic and other works. Just as trademarks are protected from the moment of their first public use, copyright is protected from the moment of creation of work.

Technological advances are the driving force behind the present trend towards greater protection for IP, the adoption of International norms and standards for the protection and enforcement of IPR will increasingly become a major component of legally binding international agreement as in the area of the TRIPS agreement. So also the various international conventions on IP, Bilateral or Regional Agreements. There is a need to take a fragmented approach to the question of protection and enforcement of IPR. The adoption of good IPR system will increasingly become an essential requirement to have an access to cutting edge technologies. There is a need to subscribe to international norms and standards. Whether out of conviction or compulsion, the IPR system has to be used to better technological progress. It is also extremely important that countries like India create a greater awareness and understanding of the issues related to the protection and enforcement of IPR in its industrial, scientific and academic communities.

In 1893, BIRPI (United International Bureau for the Protection of Intellectual Property) administered only four international treaties. Today, its successor, WIPO, administers 24 treaties (two of those jointly with other international organizations) and carries out a rich and varied program of work, through its member States and secretariat, with following missions;

- To harmonize national intellectual property legislation and procedures and
- To Provide services for international applications for industrial property rights.

ORIGIN OF WIPO

The WIPO was established in 1970 and became one of the specialized agencies of United Nations (UN) in 1974. Its origin however, seems from Paris (1883) and Berne (1886) Conventions. Both of these treaties provided for the establishment of secretariats that were merged in the year 1893 to form which the WIPO.

The WIPO is the "specialized agency of UN for inter-government co-operation in 'industry property' and "copyright" and neighboring rights". It carries out an amalgamation of activities in the field of Intellectual property, International co-operation and the transfer of technology, with special emphasis among developing countries.

OBJECTIVES AND SCOPE OF WIPO

Its purpose is to promote the protection of IP throughout the World, in resonance with the Paris Union (1883) and the Berne Union (1886). The object of the present analysis is to examine how WIPO is co-coordinating this issue of human knowledge with other multilateral treaties.

1. WIPO gives protection through

- International Agreements and
- It's Organizations.

2. WIPO's another object is to promote the development in the fields of

- Economics and Trade.

3. Various mechanisms of WIPO include the following

- It Encourages scientific research, development of new technology and industrial process and it stimulates new inventions of commercial utility.
- It is responsible for promotion of the protection of IP throughout the World.
- It encourages the conclusions of new International treaties and modernization of national legislation.

- It gives technical assistance to developing countries, assembles and disseminates information; provides services for facilitating protection of IP.
- It promotes other administrative co-operation among member states.
- A substantial part of the activities of WIPO is devoted to development and co-operation with developing countries.
- It carries out a programme of legal and technical assistance for developing countries to help them to deal with their patent, trademarks, industrial design and copyright problems.

STRUCTURE OF WIPO

The power to establish specialized agencies being intergovernmental in nature and as each government has its own constitution, structure and functions of WIPO were made under the "*United Nations Charter*". The WIPO became a specialized agency under the UN in accordance with Articles 57 and 63 of the charter of the United Nations on 17th December 1974. It has 183 member states.

The Head Office of WIPO is situated at 34, Chemindes columbetters, Geneva. The Director General is the head of WIPO.

The UN General Assembly is one of the three governing bodies that oversee WIPO and is composed of all states that are party to the WIPO convention. Once in every two years, WIPO members meet to adopt budgets and programs. All member States are represented in the conference. It meets in ordinary sessions.

Co-ordination committee is a WIPO's second Governing body. Members of this committee are elected from the member States of WIPO, the Paris and Berne unions and ex officio, Switzerland.

The International Bureau is a third governing body of WIPO. The International Bureau works as "*Secretariat*" of WIPO. It prepares the meetings of the various bodies of WIPO and the unions mainly through the provision of reports and working documents. It organizes the meetings and sees that the decisions are communicated to all those concerned and as far as possible that they are caused out. The International Bureau implements projects and initiates new ones to promote international co-operations in the field of IP. It acts as an "*information service*" and publishes reviews. It is also the depositary of most of the treaties administered by WIPO.

More than 160 Non-Governmental organizations have observer status in WIPO. There are two advisory bodies, namely,

- The policy advisory commission. It comprises eminent politicians, diplomats, lawyers and public officials.
- Second advisory body is the Industry Advisory Commission. It comprises senior business representatives.

POWERS AND FUNCTIONS OF WIPO

International organizations such as International Trademark Association (INTA) and WIPO are actively promoting the use and protection of IPR. The organization's main areas of work is to focus on strengthening the IP System of developing countries; promoting new or revised norms for the protection of IP at the national, regional and multilateral levels and facilitating the acquisition of IP protection through International registration system. One of WIPO's major activities is the progressive development and application of international norms and standards. The organization prepares new treaties concerning IP protection and undertakes the revision of the existing treaties that it administers.

INTERACTION OF WIPO WITH UN, SPECIALIZED AGENCIES AND GATT

Perhaps, no other subject has evoked so much attention, in the recent times, all over the world, particularly in developing countries like India, as the IP consequent on the coming into force of GATT Agreement and establishment of WTO. India as a signatory to the establishment of WTO, will have to make drastic changes in her ability to manage the IP be it patent, design, trademarks or copyright.

The Uruguay final act strings together 25 agreements, declarations and decisions in the goods sector alone, including the agreement on TRIMS, TRIPS, GATT and establishment of WTO. Thus Uruguay Round extends the multilateral trade to 3 new areas, namely investment, IPR and services.

WTO was setup under the provision of the Uruguay Round Global trade accord conducted in general on 15th Dec 1993. WTO was established to provide a forum for future multilateral trade negotiations, conductance of periodic review of member country trade policies and co-operation with the World Bank and the IMF. It was entrusted with right to tell a country that it violated a trade obligation and is operation would narrow the scope for unilateral action. When any country joins WTO, it must agree to accept automatically all the Uruguay Round accords without exception. The request by a member to waive an obligation under the accord will require a three fourth majority of the members. Any amendments to the accord that would effect the rights and obligations of GATT members and in turn require acceptance by two thirds of the members.

The GATT is not a single agreement, but is a series of over hundred agreements and protocols namely, TRIMS, TRIPS and TRADE IN SERVICES.

WIPO CONSIDERS IP AS A WEALTH CREATING TOOL IN ECONOMY

The Mission of WIPO is to promote through International Co-operation the creation, dissemination, use and protection of works of the human mind for the Economic, Cultural and Social progress of all mankind. In the era of globalization, the mission of WIPO is very important one because "one of the greatest challenges that WIPO faces today is the take of making the promise of IP as a tool for Economic development as a reality" (Dr. Kamilleris, Director General of WIPO).

"In this 21st century, IP is a powerful driver of economic growth. After the Second World War, the importance of technological innovations, promotion of creativity and inventiveness has increased. With the advent of globalization of economy, countries have started realizing the importance of protecting the present economic their inventiveness, wherein the role of WIPO steps in.

"IP law, considered as now a integral part of economic life" all over the world. It protects use of ideas and information's that are of commercial value. In the context of Technology revolution, it is the brain power, and not the Money. The WIPO has assumed great significance in the coming millennium on account of globalization of economy. WIPO has led to the awareness of the world with regard to IP and its protection. WIPO also maintains WIPO arbitration center, to facilitate the settlement of IP disputes between private parties. Protection was considered necessary for industrialization and investment of efforts. Two new treaties, adopted by WIPO, namely copyright and neighboring rights and WIPO performances and phonograms treaty (WPPT) have established new rights for authors, performing artists and producers of sound recording.

References

UN charter – New York

Dunkel Proposal, 20th Dec, 1991.

TRIPS Agreement of the GATT.

Paris Convention 1883.

Berne Convention 1886.

Copyright Act 1957.

Patent Act, 1970.

Intellectual Property Rights Demystified, 2008
Mu. Ramkumar & A. Jayakumar (ed.), pp. 63-76
New India Publishing Agency, New Delhi (India)
E-mail : newindiapublishingagency@gmail.com
Web: www.bookfactoryindia.com

7

Historical Evolution of Intellectual Property Protection and The Road to TRIPS

PRABHA S. NAIR
School of Legal Studies, Cochin University of Science and Technology, Cochin.

ABSTRACT

This paper provides an account on the origin of the concepts of IP, gradual development and their culmination at the TRIPS.

INTRODUCTION

Intellectual property rights form the most prominent and ever-expanding category of rights in the 21st Century. It differs from other proprietary rights in many respects and prevails in most articles of law, which influence our daily life. The economic significance of intellectual property rights has made it a subject of global political interest. In the broader sense, the term "intellectual property rights" connotes different categories of rights such as patents, copyrights, trademarks, designs, plant varieties, semiconductors, geographical indications, trade secrets and data exclusivity with varying scope and content. The reason for the existence of various categories of intellectual property rights is that the subject matter of protection is different. Patents are the exclusive rights granted to the creators of new invention. Copyrights are granted for authors of original works. Trademark protection involves rights relating to signs that individualizes the goods of a given enterprise and distinguishes from the goods of a given competitor. Industrial design refers to the rights granted to protect the original ornamental and non-functional features of an industrial article or product that result from design activity. Plant variety protection signifies the rights granted to the breeders of new and traditional plant varieties. Layout designs of integrated circuits are yet another subject matter of IP protection. Geographical indications are signs used on goods with specific geographic origin and a reputation or quality attributable to different factors of that place. Trade secrets involve rights in technical and business confidential information. Data exclusivity means rights against unfair use of test data or information containing commercial value submitted for obtaining market approval of pharmaceutical and agricultural products that utilize new chemical entities. Since the subject matter in each of these categories is different, the nature of protection also varies accordingly. They require their own minimum standards to be eligible for protection.

The intellectual property laws as we see today are definite and well structured both in the international and domestic levels. Each category has established its own subject matter, criteria and enforcement mechanism. Nevertheless, this branch of law also had a period of evolution during which uncertainty and confusion were the norms. Since the earlier forms of intellectual property protection related only to patents, trademarks, designs and copyrights, the scope of this work is also confined to them. This paper is an attempt to trace the evolution of IPR laws as a response to the socio-economic conditions prevalent at each point of time. An outline of the historical evolution of intellectual property rights will be helpful in properly understanding the present system of protection as prevailing under the TRIPS Agreement, its merits and defects. It would also be helpful in realizing the position of the developing countries in a multilateral trading regime. The paper is intended to serve as a background material for properly analyzing the implications of the TRIPS agreement in domestic and international level.

EVOLUTION OF TERRITORIAL PROTECTION

Patents

The origin of patents is mostly traced from the Europe. During the first half of fourteenth century, patents were in the form of open letter of privileges (Hulme, 1896). This was mainly to promote industrial development in England that faced stagnation as compared to continental countries like France, Germany, Italy, Spain etc. In the 14th Century, textile industry was established in England owing to the efforts of the Crown. For the growth of the textile industry, the Crown started giving various grants to foreign traders in return for establishment of industry in the Commonwealth and teaching the interested natives the art of weaving. Unlike the present patent system, this period never necessitated the invention to be new or inventive and the person who established the industry to be the true and first inventor. The protection at that time was never based on any established justifications of intellectual property. It is also to be noted that there was no need for disclosure of the invention and the sole object of granting monopoly was promotion of industrial growth (Gopalakrishnan, 1994). Though in 1611, disclosure was made a compulsory obligation for the grant of patents, the specifications never contained enough description of the invention so as to make it workable for others. Slowly, the abuse of patent monopoly started and it culminated in bringing out a new legislation, the Statute of Monopolies in 1624 that laid the foundations of the modern patent system limiting the term of protection by patents as 14 years, confining the protection to the true and first inventor and bringing in the element of novelty as a criterion for patent protection. Only in the year 1852, procedural changes were introduced in the English patent law (Thorley et al. (2000).

Soon after becoming independent from England, United States of America established an independent patent system safeguarded by legal measures initiated during the year 1787. According to that law, the Parliament would grant limited exclusive rights to inventors for a limited period (http://www.jpo.go.jp/seido_e/ rekishi_e/ rekisie.htm), the purpose of which was to promote the progress of useful technology and sciences. Based on this Constitutional provision, the US patent law was enacted in 1790. Similar developments were there in France, Germany and Turkey, etc.

Copyright

During the medieval period, the copyright privilege had nothing to do with the encouragement of intellectual creativity or originality of expression. It was in Europe during 15th Century with the advent of printing press technology, the literary property in published works got a legal recognition in terms of copyright. Before that, copying of books was mostly by hand, and for this the authors neither consulted nor paid. Italy was the first country offering copyright protection and these privileges were first in the form of exclusive privilege to conduct all form of printing in return for establishing the craft. Slowly it began to shape as monopolies in the form of exclusive licenses to print or sell an entire class of books for a stipulated term, prohibitions on importation of books printed abroad and patents for improvement of printing and typography. Authorship of books was initially not of a much concern at that time since demand was more on books like Bible. The printing technology made duplication of works easier and cheaper and publishers were the real beneficiaries of it. This had created awareness among the authors about their right of copying, giving birth to a new category of property right.

A decree issued by Venice during 1544-1545, prohibiting printing of any work without written permission from the author or his legal heirs is assumed to be the first copyright law of the World. In England, copyright was given as a monopoly franchise granted for regulating the business of printing and publishing. This was also aimed at controlling publication of literature against the King and the Church and this control was exercised through the grant of letters patent giving right to publish specified works. Later, this control was modified by giving the members of the Stationers Company the sole right to publish. Registration was compulsory for the matters published and the copies were to be given to the libraries. Though there was no express provision recognizing the rights of authors at that time in England, authors had property rights over their unpublished manuscripts, which provided contractual protection under the common law helping them to retain the form and content of the works given for publication. So though there was no copyright to the author at that time, his/her permission was needed for publishing the manuscript.

In the year 1662, the Licensing Act of Charles II was enacted recognizing the rights of authors that expressly prohibited the publication of a book without the consent of the author. But after the expiry of the term of license, the books were pirated, thereby raising the concern of authors and the subsequent hues and cry for legal protection resulted in the enactment of the Statute of Anne in 1709 as the first direct legislation in the field of copyright. The object of the Act was encouragement of learning and securing of the right of copying on the rightful owners. It set out limited terms for the enjoyment of the author's exclusive right of copying and publishing books with penal measures for violation of such rights. The mandate of registration was also retained in the Statute. Thereafter, it was only in 1842 that the Copyright Act was passed by the Victorian Parliament extending the limit of copyright after the lifetime of the author.

The development of copyright law in the United States was based on the provisions of the Statute of Anne. There was a similar development in France also and the major difference that existed between the Statute of Anne and the various decrees issued in France enforcing the copyright was that the rights were described as "author's rights" in France to be enjoyed throughout the lifetime of the author and it was not subject to any formalities such as registration. In Germany, due to the influence of some philosophical concepts, the non-economic rights of the authors were brought to the main stream and they contributed the concept of moral rights of the authors in the development of the copyright system.

Trademarks

Marks were used as early as 4000 BC to brand cattle and other animals (Diamond, 1998). Later they began to be used as indicators of ownership and origin of various goods produced (Drescher, 2000). With an increase of trade during the 12th Century, guild marks and within them, production marks originated. The function of the guild mark was to identify the cluster, which produced specific goods from other clusters engaged in the production of similar goods. Production marks within the guild system were used to identify the particular producer of goods within a particular guild and to impose liability on him for production of low quality merchandise. In the later half of 19th Century, as a result of industrial revolution and mechanized production, the whole market environment changed giving way to global markets and free competition and at this juncture, the function of the trademark changed from producer identification to product identification, advertisement and a guarantee of consistency in quality.

France made the first legislative attempt for the protection of marks by enacting Legislation Relating to Commercial Marks and Product Marks, 1857. The laws for protecting trademarks were announced in England and the USA as laws for protection against fraud followed by separate statutes in 1875 and 1870.

Industrial Designs

The beginning of industrial design protection started with the growth of textile industry when designers and printers created new textile patterns and designs (Howe, 1998). They were initially identified with copyright. A legal system protecting designs was initiated through an ordinance issued in France for the protection of ornamental designing of textile weaving industry. Similar efforts were made in US, Germany, England etc. When the goods crossed borders, the countries entered into bilateral agreements for protecting them abroad.

EVOLUTION OF INTERNATIONAL PROTECTION

Industrial revolution created an international market for literary works and mechanical inventions. When the goods that enjoyed territorial protection crossed the borders, they began to face a total anarchy. Many of the goods and works began to be reproduced abroad without permission and without receiving royalty. The position became clearer by the US Copyright Act of 1790, which granted copyright protection only to the citizens and residents of the United States. So protecting their inventions, goods and works abroad, the countries began to enter into bilateral agreements. This shift was evident in all areas of IP like patents, copyrights, designs and trademarks. Piracy of the intellectual property involved in the goods subjected to international trade was the motivating force behind the conclusion of bilateral agreements (Evans, 1996). The underlying principle of the bilateral agreement was national treatment, which means that a country will protect the works of a foreign country as the works of its own nationals. But during the elaboration of this principle, the level of protection extended by individual state was not of a much concern and only required that works be protected in the same manner as that of the nationals of the protecting country. Though this principle seemed working initially, there were many legal absurdities making the protection of foreign right holders a subject of uncertainty. Bilateral measures were exhausting, time consuming and laborious and unable to cope with the increasing economic significance of intellectual property (Katzenberger and Kur, 1996). Since the bilateral agreements were weaker in many respects, stronger protection of intellectual property was the need of the time. The reason for reluctance of foreign inventors to display their invention in the international exhibition convened by the Austrian Government in Vienna in 1873 was nothing other than the fear of piracy of their invention and the insufficient protection offered by the bilateral patent protection offered in Austria upon the principle of privity of contract (The Paris Convention for the Protection of Industrial Property). This had acted as a catalyst to the thought for evolving an international treaty for the protection of intellectual property. The bilateral agreements concluded for the protection of trademarks and designs also proved ineffective due to the same reasons. An international undertaking for the protection of industrial property became inevitable for balancing the international trading interests in light of the technological advancements. Through a series of negotiations from 1873, the call for a harmonized industrial property law by the growth of industrial production, increasing international trade and international flow of technology culminated in the enactment of the first international agreement in this regard i.e., the Paris Convention for the Protection of Industrial Property in 1883. Initially 11 States signed the Convention.

The definition of industrial property in Paris Convention is very wide incorporating patents, trademarks, service marks, appellation of origin, unfair competition and even covering agricultural and mining industries. But there is no obligation to the member countries to protect all subject matters indicated by this definition. It protects only the core subjects of patents, designs and trademarks by means of the substantive requirement concerning priority filing. The system of Convention priority provides the Member countries a priority status to application for patents, trademarks and designs in Convention countries preceding 6 months of the first application. The protection in each of the member country is independent of protection in the country of origin. Priority status permits the applicant 12 months time to complete the formalities for securing national treatment. But the substantive provisions do not mandate the countries to impose any criteria for the subject matter to be eligible for protection. The obligation under the Paris Convention is reinforced by the undertaking to enact domestically the measures necessary to ensure the application of the Convention followed by obligation to provide national treatment.

To quote Evans, "the Convention has been criticized for its inability to accommodate new subject matter and lack of capacity to enforce minimum standards of protection in Member States." Since the measures under the Paris were not stringent, it turned inadequate to enforce the rights of industrial property holders the reason being that the extent of protection in each country varied according to the strength of intellectual property laws in it. There was no scope for harmonization in the level of protection. It also lacked the remedial measures necessary for enforcement of IPR. The dispute settlement body of Paris was the International Court of Justice and the member countries were able to make its jurisdiction ineffective by declaring them to be not bound by the said provision.

The most controversial article of the Paris Convention is Article 5 providing that "importation by the patentee into the country where the patent has been granted of objects manufactured in any of the countries of the Union shall not entail forfeiture of the patent". The change introduced by this Article is quite interesting since all the developed countries used patents as tools for establishing industries in them and suddenly there occurred a shift in the argument that local manufacture cannot be insisted as a basic criterion for the grant of patent monopoly. In the first and second Revision Conferences of the Convention during 1897-1900 and 1911, this was a major issue and there were many unsuccessful attempts to ban revocation for non-working of the patented invention. Later in the Hague Revision Conference, 1925, the sanction of compulsory licensing was inserted in Article 5 instead of the term forfeiture and added that forfeiture could be exercised only when the compulsory licensing proves insufficient to prevent the abuse. It is also to be noted that non-working came to be replaced by the term abuse of monopoly giving scope for wider interpretations. It was later added that compulsory license could be permitted in the case of failure to work or insufficient working only on the expiration of 4 years from the date of filing of the patent application or 3 years from the date of grant of the patent whichever expires last and should be refused if the patentee justifies his inaction by legitimate reasons. This makes it clear that the Paris Convention was upholding the interests of import monopolies and was less favorable to the developing countries that actually wanted the working of the invention in the protecting country.

In the field of copyright also, the bilateral treaties created greater complexity due to the diversity of laws persisted (Garnett et al. 1999). At the initiation of authors like Victor Hugo, the International Literary Association was formed in 1878 in Paris. After a series of regular meetings in different parts of Europe, in 1883 in Berne, the Association produced a draft text of an international copyright agreement rooted on the principle of national treatment and producing a set of minimum rights for state recognition. Later in 1886, the Bern Convention for the Protection of Literary and Artistic Works was adopted.

The Berne Convention (1886) provided an explicit but non-exclusive list of works to be protected. Based on the principle of national treatment, it defined the conditions for protection and specified rules governing the term of protection. Protection is automatic and not based on any formalities like registration and irrespective of the existence of protection in the country of origin. The term of protection is limited to the lifetime of the author and an additional period of 50 years. In subsequent revisions, the provisions were amended to increase the scope of author's rights. In addition to the translation rights originally recognized by Berne, more exclusive rights were added in the course of revision reflecting the technological developments during the period. With respect to the subject matter of copyright, the Berne does not articulate a standard of originality and leaves it to the possibility of national variations (Ginsburg, 2000).

EVOLUTION OF GLOBAL PROTECTION

The Road to TRIPS

Though Paris and Berne conventions were in operation from 1883 and 1886 respectively, many more developing countries became signatories to those conventions only after the Second World War, especially after the independence of many nations. By the decline of colonial era, the major industrialized nations lost their traditional markets in such countries thereby new markets began to arise. It became necessary for the developed nations to protect the technology that flowed to these new markets where IP protection was absent or in the infant stage. But the newly emerged States wanted the international system accommodative of their stage of economic development and began to bargain for it. Accordingly, changes were made in the Bern allowing the developing countries to get greater access to copyright materials through the Stockholm Protocol, 1967. Paris Convention was also subject to revision in 1980, 1981, 1982 and 1984 due to the push from the developing countries for more liberalized provisions on compulsory licensing (Dhavan *et al.* 1990). Though Paris and Berne were frequently revised to adapt to the changing international scenario, there was a growing realization that due to the ineffective cross-border enforcement of intellectual property rights, developed countries were facing adverse impact on their trade revenues. To prevent the free riding, there was a suggestion to link IP with trade so that as the part of a multilateral agreement on trade, a set of IP standards could be established to be given a global coverage coupled with proper enforcement mechanism to dispute settlement. During the Ministerial Meeting at Punta del Este, in September 1986, IP was included as a negotiating issue in Uruguay Round of Trade Talks. On 15th April 1994, the Uruguay Round concluded in Marrakech with the signing of the Final Act of GATT Embodying the Results of the Uruguay Round of Multilateral Trade Negotiations. It contained a number of agreements including the agreement establishing the WTO and the Agreement on Trade Related Aspects of Intellectual Property Rights (TRIPS). The TRIPS is binding on all members of the WTO and no member can sideline the TRIPS obligations.

The TRIPS agreement

The TRIPS is founded upon the principles of territoriality and national treatment and its far-reaching effect is spread to all States who are the Members of the multilateral trading system. The previous conduct of keeping reservations while ratifying conventions and protocols is no longer permissible under TRIPS. The TRIPS obligation based on national treatment extends to all categories of IP. So it is applicable to copyright, performance rights, integrated circuits and trade secrets in addition to the categories of industrial property recognized by the Paris convention. The substantive provisions contained in the Paris and Bern conventions are retained in the TRIPS. Yet another principle on which the TRIPS operates is the principle of most-favored nation providing that any advantage, favor, privilege or immunity granted by a member to the nationals of any other country, whether a member or not, shall be accorded immediately and unconditionally to the nationals of all other members (WIPO IP Handbook, 2004). The principle of national treatment under TRIPS provides for minimum standards for the creation and enforcement of IPR among the Member States as specified herein.

"Members shall give effect to the provisions of this agreement. Members may, but shall not be obliged to, implement in their law more extensive protection than is required in this Agreement, provided that such protection shall not contravene the provisions of this agreement. Members shall be free to determine the appropriate method of implementing the provisions of this Agreement within their own legal system and practice".

It requires the States to establish a common and enlarged set of IP standards by virtue of State participation in regional and multilateral trade regimes. Compliance with the agreement is ensured through monitoring by the TRIPS Council and allotting the dispute settlement jurisdiction to the WTO dispute settlement mechanism. This TRIPS mechanism along with the vigil shown by major industrialized countries like USA and Europe for compliance by the international community makes the Agreement a legal reality. In contrast to the Paris Convention, TRIPS represents considerable erosion in national sovereignty by establishing criteria for protection. Again, it sets out the obligation of the Member States to provide procedural, administrative and remedial measures necessary for the enforcement of IPR by foreign right holders and nationals. The changes introduced by the TRIPS system could be summed up thus:

- All the provisions are binding on the Members, leaving no room for evading the obligations under the Agreement. Subject matter of protection is well defined providing an exclusive list. Criteria for protection are also specified for each category.
- Minimum term of protection to be given to each category of IP is specified in the Agreement. By coupling the principle of national treatment with most-favored nation treatment, it secures uniform international standards for the protection of intellectual property among the Members of the WTO. Procedural, administrative and remedial measures are ensured in the Agreement.
- In contrast to the earlier international efforts, it establishes a binding dispute settlement mechanism.

All these changes are to be introduced by the global community in their domestic legislations to be in conformity with the TRIPS.

The IPR, in a theory, guarantee access to information and economic development. But in reality, this does not work when we realize that there is nothing in the TRIPS, which ensures technology transfer to the providers. The provisions like compulsory licensing are unworkable owing to the poor infrastructure of developing countries. This makes local manufacture of the patented products impossible thereby retarding the economic growth of developing countries like India. The TRIPS standards also result in high price for essential commodities like food and drugs.

Conclusion

The outcome of TRIPS for India is that being an active member of the WTO, it is bound to provide equality in IPR protection to foreigners and nationals alike, which in turn may create an undue burden on the natives owing to the disparity in economy of India with that of foreign nations.

References

Dhavan, R. *et.al,* 1990 Conquest by Patents: The Paris Convention Revisited. 32 JILI. p.138.

Diamond, S.A., 1998 The Historical Development of Trademarks. 65 TMR. p.266.

Drescher, T.D., 2000 The Transformation and Evolution of trademarks – From Signals to Symbols to Myth. 82 TMR. pp.309-310.

Evans, G.E., 1996 The Principle of National Treatment and the International Protection of Industrial Property. 3 EIPR. P.149.

Garnett, K. et al. 1999 Copinger and Skone James on Copyright. Sweet & Maxwell, London, p.1126.

Ginsberg, J.C., 2000 International Copyright: From a Bundle of Copyright Laws to a Super national Code? Jour.Copyright Soc.USA. Vol.47. pp.265-287.

Gopalakrishnan, N.S., 1995 Intellectual Property and Criminal Law, National Law School of India University, pp.180-182.

Howe, Q.C.M., 1998 Russel-Clarke on Industrial Designs, Sweet & Maxwell, London, p.7.

Hulme, W., 1896 The History of the Patent System under the Prerogative and at Common Law. 12 L.Q.R. p.141.

Katzenberger, P. and Kur, A., 1996 TRIPS and Intellectual Property, in Feiedrich-Karl Beier and Gerhard Schricker, (eds.) From GATT to TRIPS – The Agreement on Trade Related Aspects of Intellectual Property Rights, VCH Publications, New York, p.17.

Thorley, S., *et.al,* 2000 Terrel on the Law of Patents, Sweet and Maxwell, London, p.5.

The Paris Convention for the Protection of Industrial Property, 1883 Article 1 Para.3.

The Bern Convention for the Protection of Literary and Artistic Works, 1886, Article 5.

WIPO Intellectual Property Handbook, 2004 (2nd edition) p.348.

www.jpo.go.jp/seido_e/rekishi_e/rekisie.htm

Intellectual Property Rights Demystified, 2008
Mu. Ramkumar & A. Jayakumar (ed.), pp. 77-96
New India Publishing Agency, New Delhi (India)
E-mail : newindiapublishingagency@gmail.com
Web: www.bookfactoryindia.com

8

TRIPS and its Implementation on IPR Regimes of Developed and Developing Nations: An Overview

T. AGITHA GOPALAKRISHNAN
School of Legal Studies, Cochin University of Science and Technology, Cochin.

ABSTRACT

This paper takes cues from the previous paper on the evolution of IPR concepts and attempts explaining the nuggets of TRIPS and analyzes the current trends in its implementation.

INTRODUCTION

As the TRIPS Agreement signifies stronger protection of conventional and new areas of intellectual property, the question that how implementation of TRIPS could influence developed and developing countries is to be addressed. The implications of such influence have far reaching consequences in terms of socio-economic development of Nation States, including geopolitical strategies and hence, a proper understanding on the plausible influence is essential. While the developed countries are interested in strengthening and expanding the horizons of intellectual property, the developing countries demand transfer of technology as *quid pro quo* for extending protection to the intellectual property of the developed world. While admitting that intellectual property has to be adequately and effectively protected for further technological advancements, an equal emphasis has to be given to the balancing of the rights of the owners of the intellectual property and its users because protection of intellectual property, or for that matter any property, is ultimately for achieving public welfare without stealing other's property. Any sovereign state, which takes care of public interest, could not be expected to respect intellectual property without receiving something in return. However, there is another view that alternatives to TRIPS in terms of unilateral pressures and sanctions and coerced bilateral agreements could be even more harmful to the developing countries (Picciotto, 2000). There are others who feel amazed as to why developing countries agreed to the globalization of intellectual property even at the cost of their sovereignty when it only benefited the US and the European Union (Drahos and Waite, 2002).

Intellectual property policy is defined as an equilibrium between reward to creators and inventors and promotion of interests of business and the public at large in securing access to scientific, technological and cultural advancements (Gervais, 1998). Unless this balance is maintained, innovation will be stifled rather than stimulated. The rationale of the patent system is to give an inventor of a new technology, the exclusive right to exploit the new technology in a specific territory, thus compensating his/her efforts on research and development. The first policy objective is thus the creation of new technology whereas the second policy objective is the diffusion of technology. This explains why the patent term is limited and not renewable. This also explains the patentability requirements such as novelty, inventive-step and utility.

It is from this angle that one has to look at the TRIPS Agreement to see how far the balancing of interests of the developed and developing countries is achieved by it.

HISTORY OF TRIPS

The idea of launching an international organization for trade was there from the time of the establishment of the Bretton Woods sisters, namely IMF and WB. The process establishing the ITO was launched in 1946 by a decision of the UN Council for Economic and Social Affairs (ECOSOC), which resulted in the signing of the text of GATT at Geneva on October 30, 1947. However, the ITO could not materialize due to opposition from the US, possibly due to a perceived fear of loss of sovereignty. The intellectual property and some other issues, which were not previously addressed by the GATT specifically, were included in its agenda since Uruguay Round of trade negotiations of GATT, which commenced from 1986.

The genesis of TRIPS negotiations lies primarily in the concern of the US and other developed countries that without a redrafting of the rules governing the relation of trade and intellectual property rights, they could not sufficiently protect their trade interests. It was estimated by the US that the proportion of total world trade, which is intellectual property related had doubled since the Second World War (Slaughter, 1990). Moreover, it was a concern of the US that its trade loss due to infringement of intellectual property rights amounted to as much as $16 billion per annum (McGrath, 1996). The then existing IP conventions were felt insufficient in providing adequate protection to intellectual property and in some cases, the standards in those conventions themselves were thought to be in need of updating. Moreover, those conventions did not provide for any mechanisms for resolving trade related disputes. However, India and other developing countries opposed the inclusion of IP Agreement dealing with substantive norms and standards within the GATT. They felt that the appropriate forum for negotiating a comprehensive code of intellectual property is the WIPO (Watal, 2001; Oman, 1994). But the developing countries were not united in their opposition and their opposition slowly died down. Watal (2001) lists out the reasons for the disunity among the developing countries thus:

- The absence of any formal mechanism such as G-77 in GATT;
- The effective use of Section 301 and other bilateral means by the US to obtain key concessions and win the silence of major developing country participants in the TRIPS negotiations;
- The differing expectations of gains in other areas of the Uruguay Round, like agriculture and textiles;
- The expectations of gains in other areas in attracting FDI through unilateral liberalization of trade policies, of which strengthened protection of IP was considered an essential part;
- The increasing complexity of the subjects for negotiations, the lack of Geneva based expertise, and the inability of the developing countries to engage constructively and effectively on a coordinated basis; and
- The diversity in legal systems and specific intellectual property laws.

The TRIPS Agreement, which formed part of the Final Agreement of GATT, is the broadest and most extensive multilateral agreement in the field of intellectual property.

TRIPS – BASIC FEATURES

The main feature of TRIPS is that it aims at strengthening of IPR protection. For example, it demands a very strong patent law. Article 27 of the Agreement, dealing with patentability, stipulates that "patents shall be available for any invention, whether product or process, in all fields of technology" and that patent rights should be "enjoyable without discrimination as to the field of technology". When Uruguay Round of trade negotiation was launched, more than fifty countries including few developing countries were not conferring patent protection on pharmaceuticals (Correa, 2000a). The TRIPS Agreement made it obligatory on all those countries to extend patent protection also to this field of technology. Similarly, countries like India recognized only process patents for food and pharmaceuticals. The Agreement requires that all inventions are patentable irrespective of whether they relate to a process or a product. Though Article 65.4 permits the developing countries to delay the implementation of this obligation for a period of ten years, Article 70.8 and Article 70.9 virtually nullified this concession. These provisions require the countries that have not made available patent protection for pharmaceutical products to grant Exclusive Marketing Rights (EMR) for a period of five years or until patent is granted or rejected, whichever period is shorter. Applications for EMR could be filed from 01.01.1995 itself. Thus, the transition period granted is in effect taken away. Moreover, some are of the view that EMR are even stronger than patents as discretion of the national patent office to grant or reject the right is severely curtailed (Watal, 2001).

In India, non working of patents locally called for issuing of compulsory licenses and "working" meant working locally and not just importing the patented inventions to India. This was considered as an essential aspect of ensuring transfer of technology. Now the provision could be so interpreted that there is no mandatory requirement that the patents are worked locally since Article 27.1 states that patents are enjoyable without discrimination as to "whether products are imported or locally produced".

Under Article 28, which deals with the rights of a patentee, along with the commonly accepted rights to prevent third parties from making, using and selling the patented product, the associated rights of offering for sale and importing have been added. These additional rights are often interpreted to exclude parallel imports, notwithstanding the footnote to Article 28, which refers back to Article 6, which clearly excludes the subject of exhaustion, whether national or international from the purview of WTO dispute settlement. Article 34, which shifts the burden of proof in case of violation of process patents, is another significant feature of the TRIPS Agreement. Under that provision, judicial authorities have the authority to order the defendant to prove that the process used to obtain an identical product is different from the patented process. This is a reversal of the burden of proof as it is normally up to the petitioner to produce evidence about the infringement of his/her patent.

Another significant provision is the unification of the minimum term of protection as 20 years. This is a term longer than which most of the countries permitted before the TRIPS Agreement.

Under the TRIPS Agreement, all WTO Members are required to grant patent to microorganisms. Though plants and animals and essentially biological processes for the production of plants and animals are exempted from patentability under Article 27.3(b), non-biological and microbiological processes for the production of plants and animals are made patentable under it. There is also an obligation on the Member countries to provide for protection to plant varieties either by patents, or by an effective *sui generis* system or a combination thereof. These provisions made countries rich in bio-diversity more concerned about the increasing rate of bio-piracy. The Convention on biological Diversity (CBD) has already recognized national sovereignty over genetic resources. In order to solve the conflict between the CBD and the TRIPS Agreement, now discussions are going on in the TRIPS Council as to the necessity of introducing the ABS regime as required by the CBD, in to the TRIPS provisions.

Another important feature is that the TRIPS Agreement sets few principles to be followed by its members based on its policy of non-discrimination. The first of these principles is the principle of national treatment. It is designed to prevent discrimination in favor of locals, a clear barrier to international trade. As per this principle, each party should accord to the nationals of other parties, treatment no less favorable than it accords to its own nationals with regard to the protection of IP. This principle is a clear indication of the extension of trade related concerns beyond the border measures of the parties deep into their domestic economic policies (Arup, 1993). This evidences the fact that developing countries are not given any special status under the Agreement. It also connotes that the territorial nature of patents is taken away by this principle.

Another principle embodied in the GATT is the Most Favored Nation (MFN) treatment. It requires the parties to afford, immediately and unconditionally, any advantage or favor, privilege or immunity granted by a party to the nationals of any other country to the nationals of all other parties.

Perhaps the key element of the power of the WTO is that it can authorize the application of trade sanctions for breach of any of its agreements, under the procedures laid down in its Dispute-Settlement Understanding (DSU). This seemingly harmless arrangement, developed as a form of political-diplomatic mediation and arbitration under the GATT, has become a world economic court in all but name.

TRIPS TO DOHA

The TRIPS Agreement resulted in strengthening intellectual property rights. According to Stiglitz (2002), though this had enabled American and other western drug companies to stop drug companies in India and Brazil from 'stealing' their intellectual property, it also resulted in rendering the life-saving drugs unaffordable to the developing world. When South Africa, with more than 5 million of its population affected by AIDS, passed the South African Medicines Act, which specifically allowed importation of patented medicine from the cheapest market, the US government and 41 pharmaceutical companies moved against the South African government. This had created a feeling of urgency among the developing as well as the developed countries for a correct interpretation of the TRIPS Agreement. Although the pharmaceutical companies finally backed out in view of the International outrage, this incident raised a question that while nobody would object to protection if IP and rewarding the efforts of R & D, it is of no use if it protects only the interests and welfare of few at the cost of lives of millions of people who could not afford to pay the patented drugs. There was also a strong case that the drug manufacturers are making exorbitant profits from their business at the cost of millions of lives in both the developing and developed countries. Joseph (2003) argues that there is evidence that amount reinvested into R&D, the *raison d'etre* behind the patents which inflates prices, is disproportionately small compared to certain non-R&D outlays.

Therefore, the TRIPS Council held a Special session in June 2001 to discuss the interpretation of the TRIPS Agreement. The developing countries resorted to the view that a restrictive interpretation of the TRIPS Agreement would unduly limit their ability to address public health emergencies such as AIDS. They argued that the TRIPS Agreement does not limit their sovereignty to address crises such as HIV/AIDS, and considered compulsory and parallel licensing as permissible objectives that do not violate the TRIPS Agreement (Gathii, 2002). They were of the view that the TRIPS Agreement has necessarily to be interpreted in view of its objectives and principles contained in Articles 7 and 8. On the contrary, the developed countries, particularly the US and Switzerland, took the stand that the only flexibility available to the developing countries is the extension given to them for implementing the TRIPS. With respect to the applicability of Articles 7 and 8 in the interpretation of the provisions of the TRIPS Agreement, they were of the view that the arguments of developing countries are thoroughly fallacious. When the TRIPS Council met on September 19, 2001, it discussed two drafts of a proposed ministerial declaration. However, a Declaration on TRIPS and Public Health was issued by a consensus of all WTO members at the Doha Ministerial meeting in November 2001. The reason for this could be attributed to the wide apprehension of bio-terror (Anthrax virus) in the US and European Union after the September 11 incident at the USA business districts and strategic locations. The anticipation of a large-scale public health emergency might be one reason that prompted the developed world to look at the issue from a more favorable angle (www.findarticles.com/p/articles/mi_qa3867/ is_200504/ai_n13638639/ print). The Doha Declaration (www.wto.org/ english/ thewto_e/minist_e/min01_e/ mindecl_ trips_e.pdf) recognized four flexibilities in the TRIPS Agreement, which could be used to combat public health crisis.

- ❒ In applying the customary rules of interpretation of public international law, each provision of the TRIPS Agreement shall be read in the light of the object and purpose of the Agreement as expressed, in particular, in its objectives and principles.
- ❒ Each member has the right to grant compulsory licenses and the freedom to determine the grounds upon which such licenses are granted.

- Each member has the right to determine what constitutes a national emergency or other circumstances of extreme urgency, including those relating to HIV/AIDS, tuberculosis, malaria and other epidemics.
- The effect of the provisions in the TRIPS Agreement that are relevant to the exhaustion of intellectual property rights is to leave each country free to establish its own regime for such exhaustion without challenge, subject to the MFN and national treatment provisions of Articles 3 and 4.

Para 7 of the Declaration, reaffirming the commitment of developed-country members to promote and encourage technology transfer to least-developed country members pursuant to Article 66.2, agreed that the least-developed country members will not be obliged, with respect to pharmaceutical products, to implement the provisions of the TRIPS Agreement relating to patent and undisclosed information or to enforce rights provided for under those provisions until 1 January 2016, without prejudice to the right of least-developed country members to seek other extensions of the transition periods as provided for in Article 66.1 of the TRIPS Agreement. Thus, Doha Round of negotiations becomes a turning point in the post-TRIPS negotiations. The importance of the Doha Declaration necessitates an inquiry in to the legal status of the Doha Declaration. Gathii (2002) has explained that the Declaration assumes legal authority in view of Article 31 §3 (a) of the Vienna Convention on the Law of the Treaties. As per the Vienna Convention, "any subsequent agreement between the parties regarding the interpretation of the treaty or the application of its provisions" shall be considered together with its context in the interpretation of the treaty. Doha Declaration, which emerged from the WTO's established practice of decision-making by consensus, is therefore, entitled to be considered a relevant interpretative tool. He feels that even if a country feels that the Doha Declaration is not legally binding, it still constitutes soft law with substantial persuasive authority that puts political pressure on governments and international institutions to comply.

TRIPS – FLEXIBILITY

Two types of flexibilities are available to the developing countries in implementing the TRIPS Agreement. The first one relates to the flexibility available with the definitions of different standards and concepts in the Agreement. The second type is the exceptions to the exclusive rights included in the provisions of the Agreement.

Flexibility in Definition

Definition of "Invention"

The TRIPS Agreement does not define 'invention'. This gives the WTO Member countries the option, within certain limits, to define the scope of patentability by using the flexibility in defining invention (Correa, 2000b). It is universally accepted that an invention is a process or a product, which is new, useful and non-obvious. Since these concepts are not defined under the TRIPS Agreement, it permits the member countries a wide range of flexibilities in retaining national standards of patentability.

Possible Exceptions to Patentability

i. Ordre Public or Morality

There is no universally accepted notion of *ordre public* and morality. Hence, the member countries are at liberty to specify which situations are covered under it, depending upon their social and cultural values. The exclusion from patentability under Article 27.2 also covers inventions, the commercial exploitation of which is necessary to protect human, animal or plant life or health or to avoid a serious prejudice to the environment.

ii. Diagnostic, Surgical or Therapeutic Methods

Article 27 (3) (a) of the TRIPS Agreement authorizes members to exclude from patentability the diagnostic, therapeutic and surgical methods for the treatment of humans and animals. However, the non-patentability referred to in this exception clause does not extend to the devices or products that may be used to apply one of the above methods.

iii. Plants and Animals

Article 27.3 (b) of the TRIPS Agreement allows member countries to exclude from patentability the plants and animals. However, it requires that plant varieties be protected either by patents or by an effective *sui generis* system.

Scope of Claims

The Agreement leaves it to the members to formulate the mode of structuring patent claims. Some counties allow broad claims. By narrowing down the claims, the wide cover of monopoly of a patent could be curtailed.

Claim Interpretation

The TRIPS Agreement does not specify how claims are to be interpreted. This is an important issue left to national legislation, since the actual scope of the rights conferred by a patent is determined by the interpretation of the respective claims under the so-called "theory of equivalents". Legislation should define inventions that are not literally described in a claim might be deemed "equivalent" and therefore considered to infringe the patent rights. Another aspect, with regard to which options are open, is the date at which equivalence is considered- whether it is filing date of the application or the date of the alleged infringement.

Exceptions to Exclusive Rights

i. Objectives and Principles

Article 7 lays down the objectives of the TRIPS Agreement as promotion of technological innovation and transfer and dissemination of technology to the mutual advantage of producers and users of technological knowledge in a manner conducive to social and economic welfare, balancing rights and obligations along with protection and enforcement of intellectual property rights.

The fact that such a provision is contained in the body of the agreement and not in the preamble heightens its status. Arguments based on the need to maintain a balance between the interests of right holders and those of the users are also justifiable under this

Article. The reference to social and economic welfare and to a balance of rights and obligations could serve to justify exceptions to exclusive rights, where the right holder has failed to participate in social and economic development or, in other words, has used his/her rights without performing his/her obligations.

The reference to "the promotion of technological innovation and to the transfer and dissemination of technology to the mutual advantage of producers and users of technological knowledge" is one of the most important principles to be followed in the agreement. This also necessitates the working of the patent to its continued protection.

Article 8, which talks about the "Principles" of the TRIPS Agreement requires the Members to adopt measures necessary to protect public health and nutrition and to promote public interest in sectors of vital importance to their socio-economic and technological development in a manner consistent with the provisions of the TRIPS Agreement, while formulating or amending their laws and regulations.

Gervais (1998) is of the view that since Article 8 is limited by the use of the phrase "consistent with the provisions of this Agreement", which was added in the last stages of the negotiations, Article 8 is essentially a policy statement that only explains the rationale for measures taken under Articles 30, 31 and 40. However, the applicability of these Articles in interpreting TRIPS provisions was clarified in the Doha Declaration. The Declaration requires that while applying customary rules of interpretation of Public International Law, each provision of the TRIPS Agreement has to be read in the light of the object and purpose of the Agreement as expressed in its objects and principles.

ii. Article 30

Though the basic objective of patent is to promote inventions, very broad patent rights/claims may hamper innovation. One way of addressing this problem is through patent exceptions. Article 30 of the TRIPS Agreement allows exceptions to the exclusive rights conferred by patents. Initial negotiations on Article 30 were difficult due to differences between the approach of the US, which did not want any exceptions to patent rights and the EC, which wanted a closed list (Watal, 2001). The EC listed three exceptions to patent rights: prior users' rights, acts done for private, non-commercial purposes, and acts done for experimental purposes, with the proviso that they take into account the legitimate interests of the patentee and third parties.

The exceptions under Article 30 should satisfy three conditions: they must be limited; they should not unreasonably conflict with the normal exploitation of the patents; and they should not unreasonably prejudice the legitimate interests of the patent owner. Under this provision, there is considerable freedom for nations to define the kind and extent of the possible exceptions to the exclusive rights of the patent owners. Different types of exceptions, which could be provided under the Article 30 include: Acts done privately and on a non commercial scale, or for a non-commercial purpose; use of the invention for research; use for teaching purposes; experimentation on the invention to test or improve on it; experiments made for the purpose of seeking regulatory approval for marketing of a product after the expiration of a patent; *bonafide* use by a third party before the application of the patent; importation of a patented product that has been marketed in another country with the consent of the patent owner, etc. Some of these exemptions are very important and could effectively be utilized by developing nations.

iii. Experimental Exception

"The adoption of an experimental exception may permit innovation based on "inventing around" or improvement on the protected innovation based on the protected invention, as well as permitting evaluation of an invention in order to request a license, or for other legitimate purposes, such as to test whether the invention works, its sufficiency and novelty (Correa, 2000a). While the experimentation exception is rather narrow in the United States, many countries explicitly authorize experimentation on an invention without the consent of the patent owner, for scientific as well as commercial purposes.

iv. Bolar Exception

Another important exception, first introduced in the US (in a legal case between Roche Products Inc. and Bolar Pharmaceutical Co. US 856, 1984) deals with the use of an invention relating to a pharmaceutical product to conduct tests and obtain approval from the health authority, before the expiration of the patent for commercialization of a generic version just after the expiration of the patent. It is also called "regulatory use" exception. The WTO dispute panel ruling on the EC-Canada patent dispute over generic drugs held valid the Regulatory Review Exception contained in S.55.2 (1) of the Canadian Law, permitting generic manufacturers (in this case of chemicals and pharmaceuticals), without authorization of the patent owner, to develop the product and submit it to regulatory authorities for market approval so that they could market the product when the patent expires (www.wto.org/english/ tratop_e/dispu_e/ cases_e/ds114_e.htm). However, a provision permitting manufacture and storage (stockpiling) of patented products before the expiration of the patents (so that they could be made available for sale immediately after the expiration of the term of patent) was struck down by the WTO Panel. Early working exceptions of this kind, which facilitate the entry of drugs into market immediately upon expiration of the twenty year period of patent protection, have been recognized internationally as means of achieving the social goal of providing low cost medicines to consumers as soon as possible, without violating either the patent or the TRIPS Agreement (Howe, 2000). The effect of prohibiting these measures is to extend the term of patent protection beyond twenty years to the length it took the competitor to engage in testing for regulatory market and manufacture for the market.

In applying Art. 30 of the TRIPS Agreement, the Panel reached the conclusion that the "stockpiling exception" does not meet the requirement that the exception should be "limited". Howe (2000) criticizes the decision of the Panel in that it was only interested in how much the rights holder might lose, not in how much the society might gain from such an exception and this had clearly overlooked Article 7 of the TRIPS Agreement which require the enforcement of intellectual property rights in a manner conducive to social and economic welfare. He felt that it also failed to consider the scope of the adjective "limited" in the light of protection of public health, an objective explicitly affirmed as legitimate in Article 8.1 of the TRIPS Agreement. However, in the backdrop of the Doha Declaration, this decision needs reconsideration.

In 2002, when India's Patent Act was amended, a new Section 107A was introduced. This section had provided for a research exemption as an exception to the general rules of patent infringement.

Parallel Imports

Parallel imports can be legally justified under the doctrine of exhaustion of intellectual property rights. As per this doctrine, the inventor is considered to have been rewarded by the first sale or distribution of the patented product and thereby exhausted his rights to further distribution with respect to them. This doctrine, in effect, permits interested persons to import products marketed by the patent owner (or trademark- or copyright-owner, etc) or with the patent owner's permission in one country into another country without the approval of the patent owner. This permits the member countries to import patented products from the cheapest market and thus could be effectively used to control the domestic market price of the patented goods. The doctrine of exhaustion of IPR was first limited to the domestic market. However, the national exhaustion principle amounts to trade restriction and contravenes the provisions of the Article XI (1) of GATT 1947. Hence, an international exhaustion doctrine is consistent with the TRIPS Agreement. Article 6 of TRIPS on exhaustion does not restrict the freedom of WTO members on the question of exhaustion intellectual property rights as long as national treatment and most favored nation treatment provisions are not violated. It prohibits the WTO members from using the dispute settlement mechanism to address this issue. TRIPS leaves the right to decide on the question "whether the importation rights should be allowed" to the national legislatures. The Agreement's recognition of the principle of international exhaustion of rights may be seen as a logical result of the process of economic globalization. The Doha declaration also has given clarification with respect to the issue of parallel imports. Through the changes introduced into Section 107 A (b) of the Indian Patent Act in 2005, parallel importation is legalized in India. This, in effect, allows importation of patented product from a country where it is sold cheaper than in the importing country.

Compulsory Licensing

Prior to TRIPS, countries throughout the world maintained legislation authorizing the grant of compulsory licenses. The terms of this legislation varied considerably. A number of countries, such as Canada and India, provided for "licenses of right" in certain areas, such as food and pharma patents, so that after a minimum time period prescribed by the Paris Convention, any person with an interest in exploiting a patent was automatically entitled to a compulsory license. It is allowed on various grounds of public interests including non-working of patents locally, failure to meet demand for the patented invention on reasonable terms and as remedy for anticompetitive practices.

However, the TRIPS Agreement does not recognize licensing of rights. Moreover, Article 27.1 of the Agreement insists that patents are enjoyable without discrimination as to the place of invention, the field of technology and whether products are imported or locally produced.

The United States attempted to challenge those provisions of Brazil's 1996 industrial property law (Law No. 9,279 of 14 May 1996; effective May 1997) and other related measures, which establish a 'local working' requirement for the enjoyability of exclusive patent rights that can only be satisfied by the local production and not the importation of the patented subject matter. Specifically, Brazil's 'local working' requirement stipulates that a patent shall be subject to compulsory licensing if the subject matter of the patent is not 'worked' in the territory of Brazil. Brazil then explicitly defines "failure to be worked" as "failure to manufacture or incomplete manufacture of the product", or "failure to make full use of the patented process". The United States considers that such a requirement is inconsistent with Brazil's obligations under Articles

27 and 28 of the TRIPS Agreement, and Article III of the GATT 1994. The request for consultations was followed by a USA request for establishment of a panel. However, the USA and Brazil reached a solution instead of pursuing the dispute under the WTO Dispute Settlement Undertaking procedures (Chensun, 2004; Lanoszka, 2003).

Compulsory licensing enables a government to use or license the subject matter of the patent to third parties without authorization of the right holder. Such use may only be permitted if, prior to such use, the proposed user has made efforts to obtain authorization from the right holder on reasonable commercial terms and conditions and that such efforts have not been successful within a reasonable period of time. This requirement may be waived by a Member in the case of a national emergency or other circumstances of extreme urgency or in cases if public non-commercial use. Such use has to be non-exclusive, non-assignable and authorized predominantly for the supply of domestic market of the Member authorizing such use; the right holder has to be paid adequate remuneration. It is to be noted that Article 31 does not attempt to specify or limit in any way the grounds upon which such licenses may be granted. Some are of the view that since the final text of Article 31 does not place any restrictions on the purposes for which compulsory licenses could be authorized, it is quite a significant achievement for the developing countries (Watal, 2001).

However, in the area of health, this provision was given a liberal interpretation in the Doha Declaration. Paragraph 4 of the Ministerial Declaration states that the TRIPS Agreement does not and should not prevent members from taking measures to protect public health. Accordingly, while reiterating commitment to the TRIPS Agreement, the Ministerial Conference affirmed that the Agreement should be interpreted and implemented in a manner supportive of WTO members' right to protect public health and in particular, to promote access to medicines for all. The Declaration reaffirmed the right of WTO members to use the provisions in the TRIPS Agreement, which provide flexibility for this purpose. For attaining the objective sought to be achieved in paragraph 4, the Declaration, while maintaining its commitments in the TRIPS

Agreement, recognized some flexibilities in the TRIPS Agreement.

Nevertheless, the issue of nations, which are without manufacturing capabilities, remained problematic. Article 31(f) of the TRIPS Agreement says products made under compulsory licensing must be "predominantly for the supply of the domestic market". However, the provision does not rule out exports. However, in practical terms, exports will be limited to countries where the product is not patented or where compulsory license has been issued to a local entity to import the product. This leaves the issue of least developed countries that do not have the generic drug manufacturing capabilities unresolved. Paragraph 6 of the Declaration, recognizing that WTO members with insufficient or no manufacturing capacities in the pharmaceutical sector could face difficulties in making effective use of compulsory licensing under the TRIPS Agreement, instructed the Council for TRIPS to find an expeditious solution to this problem.

As a solution to this, the WTO General Council in its decision on 30th August 2003 allowed any member country to export pharmaceutical products made under compulsory licenses within the terms set out in the decision (www.wto.org/ english/news_e/ pres03_e/ pr350_e.htm). All WTO member countries are eligible to import under this decision, but 23 developed countries are listed in the decision as announcing voluntarily that they will not use the system to import. However, this decision attracted much criticism since a number of conditions attached to it made the working of it an impossibility and no application was filed under it.

Conclusion

In view of the objective of protecting intellectual property, it is essential to see that a balancing of interests of the owners and users of the intellectual property is always maintained. It is in the best interests of the entire humanity that the balancing process is effectively monitored all the time, in view of the all-pervading all-powerful nature of the TRIPS Agreement and the strong implementing mechanism behind it. In a multilateral forum like TRIPS, it is not an impossibility and this is evident from the incidents, which led to the Doha Declaration in the field of public health. It is also detailed in the preceding sections of this paper that, the power game being played the developed and developing countries for the welfare of their sovereign subjects is fraught with dangers and rewards, the sum of which should be the socio-economic welfare, which in turn is yet to be achieved for many a countries like India.

References

Arup, C.J., 1993 The Prospective GATT Agreement for International Protection. 4 AIPJ 181. p. 197.

Chensun, H., 2004 The Road to Doha and Beyond. 15 EJIL. p.123.

Correa, C., 2000a Integrating Public Health Concerns into Patent Legislation in Developing Countries, South Centre, p. 11.

Correa, 2000b Intellectual Property Rights, the WTO and Developing Countries: the TRIPS Agreement and policy options. Third World Network. pp.51-61.

Drahos, P. and Waite, B., 2002 Information Feudalism – Who Owns the Knowledge Economy? Oxford University Press. p.11.

Gathii, J.T., 2002 The Legal Status Of The Doha Declaration On Trips And Public Health Under The Vienna Convention On The Law Of Treaties. Harvard Journal of Law & Technology. V.291. p. 292.

Gervais, D., 1998 The TRIPS Agreement- Drafting History and analysis. Sweet & Maxwell. p. 65.

Howe, R., 2000 Dangerous Precedents in Dangerous Times. 3 JWIP. p. 495.

Joseph, S., 2003 Pharmaceutical Corporations and Access to Drugs: The "Fourth Wave of Corporate Human Rights Scrutiny. *Human Rights Law Quarterly* v.425 p.432.

Lanoszka, A., 2003 The Global Politics of Intellectual Property Rights and Pharmaceutical Drug Policies in Developing Countries" International Political Science Review. V.181. p.189.

McGrath, M., 1996 The Patent Provisions in TRIPS: Protecting Reasonable Remuneration for Services Rendered – or the Latest Development in Western Colonialism? 7. EIPR.398.

Oman, R., 1994 Intellectual Property After the Uruguay Round. Jour. Corp. Soc. V.18. pp. 18-25.

Picciotto, S., 2000 Defending the Public Interest in TRIPS and WTO, in Peter Drahos and Ruth Mayne (eds.) Global Intellectual Property Rights: Knowledge, Access and Development, Oxfam. p. 224.

Slaughter, J., 1990 TRIPS: The GATT Intellectual Property Negotiations Approach Their Conclusion. 11. EIPR 418.

Stiglitz, J., 2002 Globalization and its Discontents. Penguin Books. p. 8.

Watal, J., 2001 Intellectual Property Rights in the WTO and the Developing Countries. Oxford University Press. p. 24-44.

www.findarticles.com/p/articles/mi_qa3867/is_200504/ai_n13638639/print.

www.wto.org/english/thewto_e/minist_e/min01_e/mindecl_trips_e.pdf.

www.wto.org/english/tratop_e/dispu_e/cases_e/ds114_e.htm.

www.wto.org/english/news_e/pres03_e/pr350_e.htm

Intellectual Property Rights Demystified, 2008
Mu. Ramkumar & A. Jayakumar (ed.), pp. 97-103
New India Publishing Agency, New Delhi (India)
E-mail : newindiapublishingagency@gmail.com
Web: www.bookfactoryindia.com

9

IPR in The Era of Globalization

A.JAHITHA BEGUM AND M.VAKKIL
Department of Education, Periyar University, Salem - 636 011.

ABSTRACT

This paper attempts to portray prevailing scenario of IPR in the light of globalization with special emphasis on harmonization of IPR systems and laws of different countries.

INTRODUCTION

The globalization of information, facilitated by the Internet, has significant implications for intellectual property regimes of national and international levels. Assessment of these implications and their probable outcomes is unavoidably value-driven. Globalization represents ever-increasing influence of developed nations and transnational entities over developing and less developed nations. The process has also brought in significant changes in understandings of sovergenity. An analysis of the implications of globalization of information on international and domestic intellectual property rights and legal regimes is a complex endeavor. An appropriate starting point seems to be to define the components of the issue: globalization, information and intellectual property. A review on the literature brings out the existence of different ideological and epistemological stances and different academic perspectives on each of these components.

GLOBALIZATION

"Globalization means different things to different people" (Bhalla, 1998). The term is used generally to refer to a phenomenon defined or measured by flows of trade and investment between countries (Bhalla, 1998; James, 1998). McChesney (1998) has described globalization as "the process whereby capitalism is increasingly constituted on a transnational basis, not only in the trade of goods and services but, even more important, in the flow of capital and the trade in currencies and financial instruments". In the context of information, globalization has been used in reference to the growing ease of information flow across borders or, perhaps, without regard to borders. Cate (1998) points out that the growth of digital information draws from and contributes to globalization: "Digital information is the ultimate example and a significant cause of globalization".

Production centers and markets are being globally networked. Networked computers and internet reduce the geographic space between creation and production. For example, they allow writers to ready text for publishing, composers to synthesize music and designers to shape products, all at their desktops but to be processed for selling at the doorsteps of consumers, all through networking of computers. Telecommunication media, like the fax and the Internet, enable teams of creators located across the globe to collaborate instantaneously across cyberspace.

Based on IP laws of USA Crews (1998) described globalization in this context thus: "the term IP is used in conjunction with the idea of establishing harmonization of intellectual property laws and their underlying concepts". Geller (1998) presents another formulation of globalization in the field of intellectual property law, referring to the influence of digital information and information technology as: "Laws of intellectual property define what is bought and sold on media and technology markets, notably works, trademarks, and inventions. Laws and treaties have traditionally been made and enforced by nation-states operating in a patchwork of territories. Now, the media and technology marketplace is being globalized in digital networks. The law is only beginning to respond to this change."

INFORMATION

Barlow (1996) opined that intellectual property rights, specifically copyrights, are outmoded and irrelevant in a digital age. According to him, information is an activity, a life form and a relationship. This conceptualization of information led him to conclude to the extent that if information is considered property, information in digital form must change the nature of property and the laws developed to protect it: He has further added that in the absence of the old containers, almost everything we think we know about intellectual property is wrong and we have to unlearn it. We're going to have to look at information as though we had never seen the stuff before.

Leith (1997) describes an increasing movement in practice, in support of characterizing or treating information as a form of property and he suggests that this movement has been carried forth into the legislative arena. He had commented "We are seeing a situation where information is becoming commodified. This commodification of information is being explicitly encouraged by various legislative bodies and property rights are being built up which, until recently, had insubstantial existence". Sassen (1998) describes the present as an era in which some are able to use information, particularly digital information, as a source of growth in both capital and power. Whether or not information can or should be described as property, it is clear that it is linked to the ability to accumulate wealth. The ease of information flow in the current digital environment and the increasing importance of information as the basis for wealth-generating activity as it seems is central to the international intellectual property environment.

INTELLECTUAL PROPERTY RIGHTS

Copyright is an intellectual property right of the author of a work, giving the author certain rights in respect of the work. These rights vary among jurisdictions but generally include the right to prevent others from copying the work, altering it, or making other than certain uses (Fair Use) of it without permission. In jurisdictions following the Anglo-American copyright law legacy, the author holds this right by virtue of having created the work and registration is not a prerequisite to holding copyright. For the period of protection, copyright in effect grants the author a monopoly on decisions relating to the work. Copyright reflects an attempt to balance incentives for creativity and production with the availability of a public domain of resources upon which future authors or creators can draw.

Possession by another, a copy of the work does not diminish the copyright of the author. However, an author can assign copyright to another. Where an author is an employee, the presumption is that copyright belongs to the employer. Whether all the rights are assignable varies, however, among jurisdictions. For example, in some jurisdictions, moral rights - those relating to alteration of the work may be waived by the author but not assigned to another. The duration of the right also varies among jurisdictions; because copyright protection is a product of legislation, the period of protection depends on domestic legislation. Such domestic legislation generally is influenced by multilateral copyright agreements, however.

HARMONIZATION

One effect that seems to be clear is that globalization and the ease of trans-border (or borderless) information flow is leading to worldwide similarities in intellectual property laws and rights. According to Drahos (1997), the global period of intellectual property is marked by a weakening, at least in relation to property, of the principles of territoriality and sovereignty. Intellectual property owners are finding that the intellectual property systems around the world are beginning to converge on the same substantive standards.

Geller (1998) suggests a need for a coherent regime of international intellectual property law and observed a gradual shift of legal framework towards this goal. He has also stated that the territorial laws of individual nation-states can no longer respond to the rate at which information flow enforces borderlessness due to interconnectivity.

As trade increases in products and services that are the subject of intellectual property protection, those holding intellectual property rights become more interested in ensuring protection of those rights outside their borders. Harmonized intellectual property regimes allow transnational corporations to internationalize the different phases of production as well as distribution and sale without jeopardizing protection of intellectual property rights. They can locate production in various states, knowing that their intellectual property will be safeguarded (Drahos, 1997). As states enter into multilateral agreements and treaties to ensure protection of intellectual property rights outside their borders, they must modify domestic law to reflect the standards of those agreements and often, the standards of competitor states.

Further and significantly, globalization is accompanied by increasingly strong intellectual property protection, internationally and on many regional and domestic fronts. In his review of Boyle's book, *Shamans, Software and Spleens: Law and the Construction of the Information Society,* Leith (1997) cites, as one of Boyle's conclusions, the fact of increasing intellectual property rights and the increasing power associated therewith: "It seems to be difficult to push back the hegemony of increasing intellectual property rights. Everyone is currently claiming 'a slice of the pie' and lawyers in practice are setting out ways in which even more slices can be got from a bigger pie." Leith suggests that more is coming within the reach of intellectual property laws "because people have stopped asking what IP is for and whether it is doing any good."

Considering international intellectual property law changes from the U.S. perspective, Crews (1998) sums up the changes thus: "The economic pressures and the growing international significance of copyright have led to new law. That new law is overwhelmingly in furtherance of expanding protection, easier protection, and longer protection. Moral rights, database protection, technological controls, extended copyrights, eliminated formalities and even restored copyrights that were long in the public domain are symptoms of a legal regime of extraordinary and rapid growth."

Crews also notes that the proponents of this expansion of intellectual property protection in the U.S., in harmonization with similar changes in Europe, cite domestic economic justifications:

"For example, the extended term of protection may generate twenty more years of commercial revenue for many economically viable works. Much of that revenue may come from foreign countries where many novels, motion pictures and other U.S. works from the early twentieth century continue to find a market. The economic argument translates not only into greater revenues for U.S. copyright holders, but also into the subsequent tax revenues, employment prospects and shareholder profits that accompany expanded business. Moreover, if those revenues are derived from foreign markets, the strengthened and longer term of protection for copyrights may also help shift the balance of international trade in favor of the United States."

In contrast to the economic and domestically pragmatic arguments, Crews sees several respects in which strengthened intellectual property rights do not include a corresponding balance of the public interest. Recognizing that, in its origins, copyright law was intended to achieve a balance between preserving a public domain or commons of ideas and providing incentive for creative endeavors, he suggests the former is neglected in the trend toward the maximalist approach to intellectual property rights. For example, increased protection of necessity is accompanied by limitations on the scope of the public domain and a reduction in affordable resources available for new creators, whether individuals or corporate. Crews also cites potential limitations on the application of fair use doctrine as a consequence of a focus on greater intellectual property protection. Other consequences are: potential limitations on technological advancement resulting from restrictions on use and loss of learning opportunities resulting from restrictions on dissemination or public performance of works.

Conclusion

There are different ways of understanding the issue of the implications of globalization of information on intellectual property laws and these derive from different ways of understanding the central concepts. The literature of recent years is replete with discussion of globalization and the growth of digital information and the influences of these developments on domestic and international IP regimes.

A clear effect of globalization of information is a trend towards harmonization or standardization of intellectual property laws in the direction of greater protection. Whereas, this trend might appear to relate to positive economic effects, the literature of recent years suggests that these effects may be positive primarily for intellectual property producing nations and transnational corporations. It may also be diminishing the sovereignty of states in favor of the strength and power of private entities. It is possible that the prevalence of such writings in the literature is a response to the movement toward harmonization and stronger intellectual property protections - an attempt to ensure some of the less heard voices are expressed.

References

Aoki, K., 1988a. "Considering multiple and overlapping sovereignties: Liberalism, Libertarianism, national sovereignty, "Global" intellectual property, and the Internet," I*ndiana Journal of Global Legal Studies,* volume 5, number 2, at http://ijgls.indiana.edu/ archive/ 05/02/aoki.shtml, accessed 7 January 2002.

Aoki, K., 1998b. "Neocolonialism, anticommons property, and biopiracy in the (not-so-brave) new world order of international intellectual property protection, "*Indiana Journal of Global Legal Studies,* volume 6, number 1, at http://ijgls.indiana.edu/archive/ 06/01/aoki.shtml, accessed 7 January 2002.

Asian Dub Foundation, 2002. Colour Line. On Community Music [CD]. London: London Records 90 Ltd.

Barlow, J.P. 1994, "Economy of ideas: A framework for patents and copyrights in the Digital Age" Wired, vol. 2, number 3 (March), pp.84-90, 126 – 129, at http://www.wired.com/wired/archive /2.03/ economy.ideas_pr.html, accessed 7 January 2002.

Barlow, J.P., 1996. "Selling wine without bottles: The economy of mind on the global net, "In : Lynn Hershman-Leeson(editor). Clicking in: Hot links to a digital culture, Seattle : Bay Press, pp. 148 – 172.

Bhalla, A.S., 1998. "Introduction," In: A.S. Bhalla (editor). Globalization, growth and marginalization. Ottawa: IDRC, pp. 1-12.

Intellectual Property Rights Demystified, 2008
Mu. Ramkumar & A. Jayakumar (ed.), pp. 105-112
New India Publishing Agency, New Delhi (India)
E-mail : newindiapublishingagency@gmail.com
Web: www.bookfactoryindia.com

10

Impact of Enforcement of IPR on Developing Countries

A. VINAYAGAMOORTHY
Department of Commerce, Periyar University, Salem - 636 011.

ABSTRACT

This paper is an attempt to analyze the plausible impacts on the economy and social issues of developing countries with reference to enforcement of IPR.

INTRODUCTION

From commodity based nature, business has changed during the past hundred years in a way that ideas and knowledge have taken higher value than commodities. Today, many companies find their most valuable assets being intangible and they are therefore dependent on functioning IPR systems. But does the rigid protection of IPR serve all the people in our globalized world? The purpose of this paper is to discuss the impact of the introduction of IPR protection on developing and under developed countries in the light of TRIPS Agreement.

INTELLECTUAL PROPERTIES

Intellectual Properties as defined in other papers of this volume, are used not only in business transaction, but also in service and trade. The advent of technology stimulates the research and development, which again have a direct impact on the recognition of intellectual property. Research and creation of IP are directly proportionate to the business growth. Hence, protection of those intellectual properties is essential. Effective protection of intellectual property rights thwarts unwanted copying and spreading and thus, negative growth of economy. The brands, logos, designs, internal systems, documents and confidential matters have more value than the value of fixed assets used by the enterprises. They are long-term assets of the firm and provide higher ROI (return on investment) than other types of assets. IPR laws promote monopoly and create special policy for developing new products and service line as supplementary to the existing products or services, which again influence growth of trade and economy. If not properly regulated, monopoly of IP rights encourages piracy, leading to economic degradation. With the evergrowing awareness on the benefits of protection of intellectual properties, the need to modernize management systems for the purpose of embarking on new benefit areas has to be perceived. Thus, protection of IPR forms a core part of the business.

THE IMPACT OF TRIPS ON DEVELOPING COUNTRIES

The term 'developing country' is not clearly defined by the WTO. Instead, member-countries declare themselves as developing country. According to the WTO, the developing country status grants those nations transitional periods of up to five years for the implementation of the Trade and IP related agreements. If these countries had no protection of product patents in certain technological areas before they signed TRIPS, they are granted an additional five-year period. Least developed countries have a transitional period of 11 years. It is expected from these developing and least developed countries that within this transitional period, they make suitable amendments in their legal system for better protection of IPR, in tune with their obligations under TRIPS.

Many developing countries have had or have to change their IPR regime to fulfill the TRIPS Agreement's requirements.

Many believe that long-term benefits, namely the protection of domestic inventions and the augmentation of innovative spirit may result by adhering to TRIPS. Governments in developing countries have to find a balance between the need to protect intellectual property and the requirement to diffuse certain technologies in order to increase welfare. As per the covenants of WTO, on enforcement of TRIPS agreements, domestic output of developing countries and employment of producers of counterfeit goods will decrease. Employment, wages and tax receipts will shrink and governments of these countries will have to invest largely in administrative resources to enforce changed legislation.

Developed countries reason that the increased worldwide protection of IPR would stimulate technology and investment flows. However, the present situation looks quite different. The developing countries suffer from welfare losses while developed countries could boost their exports. Furthermore, despite all confirmations, many developing countries, which signed the TRIPS Agreement and fulfilled the WTO requirements, still are confronted with unilateral retaliation measures.

It is a fact that valuable knowledge is primarily in the hands of enterprises in the developed countries and developing countries have to import this know-how. The UN states that stronger protection of IPR will inevitably lead to increased royalty payments of licensees of technical knowledge and higher prices due to the monopoly-like position of the foreign title holder.

Developing countries are concerned that a strengthened, worldwide IPR system may lead to anti competitive tendencies with negative effects on welfare in these countries. Transnational corporations may abuse their monopoly power, gained through their intellectual property, or the transfer of technology may be restricted. Prime objective of TRIPS Agreement was not the battle against counterfeiting and piracy but "Technological protectionism". Developed countries are regarded as innovators and suppliers of products whereas developing countries serve as markets. Especially in the US, strong industrial lobbies such as the pharmaceutical and software companies earn high returns on Research and Development

(R & D). For Example, US Pharmaceutical industry claims to lose $500 million a year in India due to the country's bad IPR protection. On the other hand, in 1998, the United States received royalty payments of $36 billion. In view of this, it is plain that stronger patent protection is mainly in the interest of the industrialized counties. In 1990 only 4% of World R & D expenditures came from developing countries, which makes clear who will benefit most from strengthened IPR regimes.

Now, answer should be found for the question that why developing countries finally agreed to TRIPS. Two factors might have influenced the decision of many developing countries, to have themselves agreed to TRIPS; namely,

- Threat of bilateral initiatives by the United States.
- Developing countries saw some advantages in tariff reductions of agricultural products, textiles and other products of their concern through WTO Agreements but under the 'single package' system they had to agree to all negotiated points including TRIPS.

FOREIGN DIRECT INVESTMENT (FDI)

This form of investment would be the greatest benefit for developing countries, since they could catch up with their technological development. The developed nations described stronger IPR regimes in developing countries as the basis for an increase in FDI, but there is no evidence that there is a positive correlation without additional measures. The requirement of TRIPS that patent protection has to be ensured even if a product is just imported and not locally produced will hamper more FDI in developing countries. As a consequence, countries can be supplied with finished products, which are protected but produced elsewhere. Developing countries, in particular, will not benefit from this form of foreign direct investment or transfer of technology.

THE PHARMACEUTICAL INDUSTRY AND TRIPS

From a scientific point of view, the treatable infectious diseases, account for 14 million deaths each year, most of them in developing countries. A number of factors worsen the situation in these countries, e.g. poverty and lack of access to health services. Efficient and affordable medicines could cut down this death toll if people have access to such drugs. 25 million people out of the 36 million who are infected with HIV worldwide live in sub-Saharan Africa and the enormous share of infected people of the whole population has a dramatic impact on life expectancy in this region. Again, affordable medicines could help. In developed countries, life-saving drugs have raised life expectancy of HIV infected people dramatically but this treatment is unaffordable for people in developing countries.

The high prices of medicines are the result of patents, which give their holders the right to restrict competition and therefore sell a certain drug in a monopolistic environment. TRIPS require many developing countries to enforce their patent protection, which will restrain innovation and information flows. Moreover, prices of medicines will continue to rise, making access more difficult and destruct local pharmaceutical industries. *(The higher R & D expenses cited as reason for higher cost of medicines by the pharmacological companies is not justified as only the 15.2 % of the additional revenue earned by the companies go to R & D spends, a whopping sum of 30 % goes to marketing expenditures! The provision of TRIPS to thwart such conditions of unbearable cost of essential medicine, in terms of "Compulsory Licensing" and is being enforced by few countries such as Brazil and Thailand may help lessen the economic burden of being compliant to International treaties and conventions of IPR).* Production of generic equivalents to expensive, branded drugs will be limited because of the 20- year patent protection for pharmaceutical products and processes. In pre-TRIPS times, many developing countries, including India did not grant product patents but process patents for pharmaceuticals, enabling domestic researchers to develop similar products through a process called reverse engineering. The implementation of TRIPS put an end to this practice and fears are growing that through the timely shift of product and process application or minor changes of the ingredients of drugs, protection for medicines may be extended to long periods.

BIOPIRACY

Third World countries heavily rely on domestic agricultural production, which makes IPR in the form of "plant breeders' rights" an important issue. Three criteria have to be fulfilled in order to obtain a 15-20 year protection; the variety has to be distinct, uniform and must keep its characteristics upon reproduction. Plant breeders' rights are applied in the case of the development of new plant variety through conventional methods and the resultant process enjoys a kind of *sui generis* protection, which does not include re-using of the seed and further research based on the developed variety. The export of agricultural products and biopiracy is a dangerous threat to farmers in the developing countries. Biopiracy describes the situation where someone, either an individual or a corporation, gains a patent on a plant variety already in use by someone else. The Rural Advancement Foundation International (RAFI) points out that the victims of such action will be farmers in developing countries and the perpetrators are mostly companies in industrialized nations. As a consequence, the title holder may prevent importation of the product in question or demand royalty.

TERMINATOR CROPS

Terminator or Traitor seeds are genetically modified to be sterile and not usable for replanting. Consequently, farmers using these seeds would be forced to purchase new grain during every sowing season. This makes quite clear how dangerous Terminator technology is, primarily for the 1.4 billion people worldwide who heavily rely on farm-saved seed and who could not afford to buy new seed every year. Moreover, this technology could be used to develop plants, which may be dependent on chemical treatment in order to become fertile or healthy giving Gene Giants the power to control agriculture and thus food supply worldwide. The US ignores experts' warnings and is actively involved in the further development of a technology aimed at exploiting the poorest of the poor. The patentability of Terminator technology not only legitimates but also even fosters further research in this field, which will lead to the commercial application and adverse consequences for millions of people in near future.

Conclusion

Intellectual property rights form the basis for scientific and economic development because they offer an incentive to someone, either individuals or organizations, to invest time and knowledge in research activities. Inventors are given the right to derive monopoly profits, which means that only they are allowed to exploit their invention during a certain period of time. As a consequence, this exclusive right has to be legally enforceable. The whole society should benefit from these works, as they drive economic growth and technological development. Admittedly, the effects of IPR depend on various economic variables such as the social value or the existence of substitutes.

To summarize the situation, developing countries are bound to loose if they try to comply with the obligations imposed on them by the TRIPS. The author sees an urgent need for a reform of TRIPS in order not to discriminate against developing countries, their economies and their people.

Acknowledgements

Author thanks the University authorities and editors of this volume for having extended moral and academic support.

References

Correa, C., 2006 Intellectual Property Rights, the WTO and Developing Countries: The TRIPS Agreement and Policy Options, London: Zed Books.

Fink, C., 2006 Intellectual property Rights, Market Structure, and Transnational Corporations in Developing Countries.

Messner, Sophie., 2001 "Implications of the TRIPS – Agreement under the GATT for Developing Countries".

Pass C, Lowes B, and Davies L,. 1999 Collins Dictionary of Economics, 2nd ed. Glasgow: Harper Collins Publishers.

RAFI., 2001a USDA says Yes to Terminator, 2 November 2001.

RAFI., 2001b New Terminator Patent Goes to Syngenta, 2 November 2001.

RAFI., 2001c Enola Bean Patent Challenged, 2 November 2001.

United Nations., 1996: The TRIPS Agreement and Developing Countries. Geneva: United Nations publication.

Watal, J., 1999 Intellectual Property Rights and Agriculture: Interests of Developing Countries. Retrieved: 25 October 2001.

WTO., 2001a The WTO in brief, Retrieved: 27 October 2001.

WTO., 2001b The Multilateral trading system-past, present and future, Retrieved: 27 October 2001.

WTO., 2001c Intellectual Property Protection and Enforcement Retrieved: 27 October 2001.

WTO., 2001d who are developing countries in the WTO? Retrieved: 27 October 2001.

Intellectual Property Rights Demystified, 2008
Mu. Ramkumar & A. Jayakumar (ed.), pp. 113-127
New India Publishing Agency, New Delhi (India)
E-mail : newindiapublishingagency@gmail.com
Web: www.bookfactoryindia.com

11

Issues and Implications of IPR : A Review

T.RAMAKRISHNA
IPR Chair, National Law School of India University, Bangalore.

ABSTRACT

This paper discusses IPR concepts in the light of Indian culture and issues emanating from enforcement of those concepts in developing countries such as India.

INTRODUCTION

The adage "Knowledge is wealth" suits the present era well than any other period. India is known for its innovative thoughts since ages. However, it never monopolized the knowledge it possessed. In India, the knowledge of a person is thought to be utilized for the benefit of the society as an obligation of the knowledge holder. Does this mindset of Universal humanity (*Vasudevo Kudumbagam*) and common good (*Sarva Sugino Bavandu*) would benefit us in the materialistic society? This paper is an attempt to answer this query.

Keynote address delivered during GED-IPR 2006.

THE PAST

Intellectual Property is the creation of human intellect. 'Man' 'manush' interpreted as meaning mind and 'to think' leads to creation of product that might become subject matter of protection. A person acquiring right owns. Ownership of property in ancient India was indicative of the quality of being used according to pleasure [*"yathesta viniyogah tava chedako dharma swathva mithi].* Property to be given a liberal and wider connotation and should be extended to those well-recognized types of interests which have the insignia or characteristic of property right. Hence it is a legal concept and is the sum of a bundle of rights.

Robert M. Sherwood said: 'although largely invisible, an Intellectual Property system which protects innovation and creative expression may be viewed as a helpful precondition to creating and using new technology which boosts economic growth and aids development. From this point of view, Intellectual Property protection system may be considered as a valuable part of a country's infrastructure'. The need to expand our knowledge and to improve our technological development and dominance require a greater availability of technological information through growth and development of patent system.

A strong Intellectual Property system is primarily in the interest of nationals. The genius and creative person needs to be nurtured. Where national talent and inventiveness are neglected, inventors and scientists would go in search of a system to protect adequately their inventions and creations or move out of the nation in search of greener pastures that provide incentives to their inventiveness, which in turn, in long term, would deprive economic prosperity of their home country.

At the time when Robert Louis Stevenson was writing Treasure Island, John and Emily Roebling were completing construction of New York's Brooklyn Bridge, (i.e in the year 1883) during while a Convention for the protection of the Industrial Property was adopted at Paris. This was the result of the concerted efforts ten years after foreign exhibitors refused to attend the International Exhibition of Inventions in Vienna in 1873 being apprehensive of their ideas likely to be stolen and exploited commercially in other countries. The Paris convention enabled the protection of intellectual creations in the form of patents, trademarks and industrial designs in other countries. For the protection of the right to control and receive payments for the use of the creative works such as novels, short stories, poems, plays, songs, operas, musicals, drawings, paintings and architectural works at the international level, an international convention called as Berne Convention for the Protection of Literary and Artistic works was concluded in 1886.

With the coming into existence of the World Trade Organization, the Trade Related aspects of Intellectual Property Rights [TRIPS] Agreement imposed obligation on its members to provide the minimum protection to the Intellectual Property it recognized. The different Intellectual Property Rights recognized under the TRIPS are: Copyright and Neighboring rights, Patents, Trade Marks and Service Marks, Industrial Designs, Geographical Indications, Lay out designs for integrated circuits and protection of undisclosed information. The Agreement provided for cross-border measures for the enforcement of the Intellectual Property Rights. The World Trade Organization Dispute Settlement System provided a mechanism to settle the disputes as to interpretation and implementation of the TRIPS provisions.

The World Trade Organization [WTO] and the World Intellectual Property organization [WIPO] are the two important International Organizations administering Intellectual Property related treaties. The members of the Paris and Berne conventions have set up respective International Bureau to carry out administrative tasks. The two Bureau set up under the two conventions were united in 1893 to form BIRPI [United International Bureau for the protection of Intellectual Property]. The BIRPI moved from Berne to Geneva and later underwent structural changes to transform itself into WORLD INTELLECTUAL PROPERTY ORGANISATION [WIPO] and to become the specialized Agency of the United Nations. WIPO administers 23 Treaties as against four treaties being administered by BIRPI.

Intellectual Property has been considered as one of the human rights under Article 27of the Universal Declaration of Human Rights

1948: “Everyone has the right freely to participate in the cultural life of the community, to enjoy the arts and to share in scientific advancement and its benefits and everyone has the right to the protection of the moral and material interests resulting from any scientific, literary or artistic production of which he/she is the author”.

THE PRESENT

Intellectual Property has historically been and continues to be a major and indispensable element in the progress and development of all human kind. From earliest tools of prehistory, through the wheel, the Chinese abacus and printing press, Syrian astrolabe, the telescope, the harnessing of electricity the internal combustion engine, penicillin, the computer and countless other innovations, it has been inventiveness of the world’s creators that has enabled humanity to advance to today’s levels of technological progress and sophistication in quality of life. Inventions have been given patent protection. Patent system is the process of obtaining disclosure of information from inventor as a *quid-pro-quo* to grant of monopoly for a specified period. For grant of patent, the invention shall be required to pass through the five recognized filters: Patentable subject matter, Utility, Novelty, Non-obviousness and the Written description.

In view of the enormous expenditure involved in the Research and Development in various technologies, especially the high technology areas of Space technology, Information technology, Biotechnology, Nanotechnology, Biopharma and others, creation of exclusionary rights becomes absolute necessity. This necessitates the creators and innovators to recoup their investment and then to make profit, while making fruits of invention available to the public.

The Microsoft used as many as 5000 skilled personnel and ensured the writing of 30 million lines of code to update its 1998 version to 2000 version. Calculated in terms of the time, intellectual inputs and the investment that has gone into it, it is beyond ordinary imagination. Under these circumstances, it would not be fair to oppose the practices enforced against piracy of this software under the guise of opposing monopoly. Similarly, an investment of approximately 800 million. U.S. Dollars for bringing a molecule to the market after conducting the Research, clinical trials etc., it would not be proper to advocate free availability of the methods to produce it to all those who want to produce it by copying the method and market the product for benefit. Nor the author is not of the opinion that the law should encourage profit-oriented activities only or not in favor of the counterfeiting and imitation of the products of the innovators who would have spent lot of time, intellect and investment. If violations are allowed, the incentive to invent would die and adversely affect progress and development.

INDIAN SCENARIO

From the earliest rituals of prehistory, through the beginnings of music and dance, burial rites, cave paintings, the written word folklore and theatrical representation to the use of the modern technologies such as the phonogram, celluloid film, wireless broadcast, software and digital recording, the humankind has identified and defined itself through cultural creativity and expressions thereof in the form of artistic creations and performances, which are described as Intellectual Property. This has been brought under the realm of Copyright according to Indian law. The increased variety of copyright works has developed in an astonishingly large scale. It is a moot point whether the objective of copyright law remains to be encouraging the expressional freedom or has the interest of trade and wealth maximizing attained priority. Is the Indian cultural ethos of orienting the social policy to the cause of knowledge system eroded? TRIPS has included new technological means of expressions such as computer programs and databases and the post TRIPS WCT [WIPO Copyright Treaty] and WPPT [WIPO Performers and phongrams Treaty] have all provided for the effective regulation of the rights of the creators in the non-digital as well as digital environment.

We may have to look at the Indian patent system and how law had to be altered in the light of India's membership to WTO [TRIPS]. In India, the patent for an invention has been the creation of the statutes. The Act VI of 1856, granting exclusive privileges to inventors of new manufacture for a period of 14 years was the first legislative enactment on Patents in India. After the recommendations of the Justice Rajagopal Ayyangar Committee, the Patent Act of 1970 was adopted. This Act abolished product patents for drugs and medicines, food and certain classes of chemicals, declared certain inventions to be non-patentable, provided for the procedure for obtaining patent and had provisions for grant of Compulsory licenses. The process patent regime thus introduced had helped the domestic pharmaceutical companies to reproduce and market new drugs by adoption of a different process, in a short span of time. As a consequence, the production cost of the pharmaceutical product in India was less thereby ensuring the availability of the drugs at an affordable price.

TRIPS obligated members under Article 27 as follows: Patents shall be granted for any invention, whether products or processes provided that they are new, involve an inventive step and are capable of industrial application and also that patents shall be granted in all fields of technology. No discrimination is allowed with respect to the place of the invention or based on whether the products are locally produced or imported. It provided that the member state may exclude from patents the diagnostic, therapeutic and surgical methods of treatment for humans or animals, as well as plants and animals and essentially biological processes, except microorganisms. The member states may provide either patent or effective *sui generic* protection to the plant varieties. However, the TRIPS has also provided certain flexibilities within itself. The objective clause under Article 7 states that the objective of protection and enforcement of IPR should contribute to the transfer and dissemination of technology in a manner conducive to social and economic welfare and to a balance of rights and obligations. It is further provided under Article 8 that members in amending their laws may take measures to protect the public health and nutrition. Article 31 provided for invoking the compulsory licenses shield/sword in cases of national emergencies/extreme urgency although this is regarding the supply for domestic markets.

While recognizing the importance of IP protection for development of new medicines, the DOHA declaration of 2001 stated that member countries should have discretionary right to grant compulsory licenses and the freedom to determine the grounds of Compulsory licenses and what constitutes national emergency/ extreme urgency. It also realized the fact that many developing countries are having insufficient or no manufacturing capabilities and hence this discretionary right is essential.

Indian Patent Act was amended thrice after the TRIPS, incorporating the obligations under the TRIPS. India was forced to bring about the first amendment after the ruling of Appellate Body of the Dispute Settlement Body of the World Trade Organization that acceptance of the applications for product patent under the mail box system did not in itself comply with obligations of providing for the Exclusive Marketing Rights as a transition measure. The first amendment provided for filing applications for product patents for inventions relating to food, medicine and drugs, as also for filing applications for grant of exclusive marketing rights to sell and distribute the article subject to certain conditions. By the second amendment, changes such as definition of invention, inventive step, additional list to non-patentable inventions such as inclusion of microorganism, exclusion of invention, which in effect is traditional knowledge, exclusion of plant and animals, varieties, and medical procedure were made. The third amendment to the Patent Act brought about major change to the Indian Patent system.

To facilitate the filing of patents over microorganisms, India signed the Budapest Treaty on the International Recognition of the Deposit of microorganisms in the year 2001. As a result, an International Depository Authority was set up at Institute of Microbial Technology, Chandigarh, which is called Microbial Type Culture Collection and Gene Bank (MTCC). The Depository accepts deposit of microorganisms from patent applicants and gives them an accession number. It also conducts viability testing. The Depository works under the auspices of WIPO as an international authority for receiving deposits for Indian and international filings.

Through the amendments, the scope of patentable subject matter under section 2(j) was modified from "art, process, method of manufacture, machine, apparatus or other article or substance produced by manufacture" to "product or process", thus widening the scope of subject matter eligible for patent protection. As it stands today, the Manual of Patent Practice and Procedure released by the Indian patent office in 2005 provides very clearly in Annexure I (Examination guidelines for Biotechnology Inventions) that genes, plasmids and so on and processes related thereto would fall within the scope of patentable subject matter. The broad scope of amended definition allows patents on all biotechnology inventions except those excluded under section 3.

Section 5 which gave only process patent protection for drugs and food materials has been omitted from the Patent Act by the 2005 amendment. As a result, drugs are eligible for both process and product patents in India. The Biopharma sector, which occupies about sixty to seventy percent of the biotech industry in India, has received the impetus necessary from the patent regime from this amendment.

Changes were made to Section 25 and Section 64, which deal with opposition and revocation. Non-disclosure of source of biological resources and existence of traditional knowledge related to the invention are now valid grounds for opposition of grant of a patent or revocation of a granted patent. These provisions ensure that patents are granted to novel inventions and assure sharing of benefits with traditional communities. Similarly, Section 107A, which is similar to Hatch-Waxman Act of USA was introduced in the 2002 amendment. This section allows generic companies to use patented drugs for getting drug approval from the Drug Controller General of India. It also allows biotech companies to conduct pre-clinical and clinical studies on patented inventions as long as such activities fall within the scope of collecting information to be submitted to a government authority.

Another area where patent protection is invoked by the developed countries is the computer software development. Indian patent law has excluded expressly the computer program *per se*. It has also excluded the business method patents. The United States of America patent Office has been granting the patent protection for software that gives rise to useful, tangible and concrete result.

In United Kingdom and European Union, the position is substantially the same as in USA where the application for patenting of a data processing system used to display information in windows in such a manner that the information in one window moved automatically to a new position, when obstructed by another window. The Patent office rejected those claims pertaining to software stored on a medium that was readable by a computer, on the ground that no claim to a computer program itself be patented. The Board held that technical effect could not be said to lie merely in the fact that programs were used to operate computers, but it may be found in the further effects deriving from the execution by the hardware of the instructions given by the program [IBM/Computer program case 1999].

The patenting of one-click method of Amazon.com, the HUB-SPOKES method of calculating of the mutual funds [in State Street Bank Case] and a host of other business methods are subject matter of patents in US. The European Patent Office (EPO) has declared business methods as not "technical" and has excluded it from patentable subject matter. The EPO has clearly indicated that claim over purely business method having nothing to do with an apparatus for implementing the method will be rejected as business method as such and the claim related to the apparatus for implementing the business method will be tested for the requirements of the patentability. If computer program or business method 'as such' is given this interpretation, it could be persuasive for the Indian Patent Office as well as Indian Courts.

Computer software has been subject matter of copyright law. India has also provided for registration of the software for copyright protection. The Courts in USA and UK have evolved the test of Abstraction, Filtration and Comparison to determine the infringement of copyrights. But the deplorable part is that the software piracy has been at its peak in view of the lack of enforcement measures. As we know software piracy could partake any of the forms such as: *softlifting*-noncommercial copying and distribution through end user sharing; *counterfeiting*-illegal copying and sale as genuine software; *hard disk loading*-as incentive to potential customers; *Original Equipment Manufacturer Piracy*-

software legally sold with hardware is separated from hardware and sold; *commercial use of non-commercial software*; *internet piracy*-either through electronic bulletin board serviced, auction site piracy, file transfer protocol etc.

Recalling the example of Microsoft, a question arises. Should this piracy be tackled or allowed to dominate? In India, software is being considered as 'literary work' under the copyright law. As such, rights of the copyright owner have been conferred on the owner of software and he/she is entitled to both civil and criminal legal remedy. At the same time, we find unabated audio and video piracy. Both cinematograph film as well as sound recording has copyright protection as long as they are original. If they are original, they can approach administrative and judicial machinery to thwart piracy. However, for reasons best known to these agencies and authorities, the foul play continues.

With the rise in internet activities, in the field of e-commerce, entertainment and information and knowledge exchange, the Intellectual Property system becomes crucial. There are equally complex challenges along with the great opportunities. WIPO has come out with "Digital Agenda" to formulate appropriate responses that encourage dissemination and use of IP and ensuring protection of the rights; aiming to integrate developing countries and countries in transition into the internet environment; aiming at dispute resolution and need for effective online systems to resolve disputes.

In this era of Internet, the effective protection of the creative contents and the owner's rights is a challenging issue. The Digital Rights Management techniques developed through the WIPO treaties and adopted in the developed countries, especially the DMCA (Digital Millennium Copyright Act) of USA is noteworthy. Digital Rights management entails the operation of a control system that can monitor, regulate and price each subsequent use of a digital file that contains media content or software. Electronic access can be administered through rendering software tied to a protected work and can be complemented with encryption, digital signatures, watermarking or hardware programming. The Technological Measures could be implemented through access control, control of certain users, integrity protection, usage metering, and electronic copyrights management. The (DMCA) Act of USA prevents circumvention of Technological measures taken for protection of the IP or the digital rights. It also prohibits a person from manufacturing, importing, offering to the public, providing or otherwise trafficking in any technology, product, service, device, component or part thereof that is primarily designed or produced for the purpose of circumventing a technological measure.

The liability of the Internet service provider with scope for safe harbor is an important step in regulation of the rights on the internet. The action against Napster by the Recording Industries Association of America and the decision of the court holding Napster liable for contributory infringement is a typical example. The Information Technology Act of India provides for liability of Internet Service Providers for an act done with the knowledge of infringement. There is a need for strengthening our law for effective protection of rights of the creators.

The use of Trademarks was known to India since Indus civilization period when seals designating the source of a product were affixed on different products. In the highly integrated economy of Modern World, domestic and international trades heavily rest on identification of the product through the brands. Brand sells. Creators of brand nurtured by the customers the brand associates and in particular brand loyalists—have ultimately create goodwill. The trademark law of India protects the brands/trade/service marks. According to this law, any act likely to cause confusion or dilute the distinctiveness of trademark can be a ground for infringement action.

However, with the advent of computer era, the protection of trademark became complicated when a popular trademark was included as part of the domain name and registered by a third person to exploit the potential of using the same in the electronic space/ cyber space. Domain Names are the alphanumerical Internet Protocol [IP] addresses to designate a user computer. With the increase in cyber-squatters, law of trademark / passing off was extended to tackle them. The WIPO has been able to resolve thousands of domain name disputes. Indian Courts have addressed these issues and resolved the dispute in cases relating to registration of yahooindia.com, radiff.com, bisleri.com, drreddyslab.com and siffy.net. The interest of the customers and the owners of the trademarks are thus safeguarded.

The concept of Industrial Design and the IP can be noticed from first industrial designs of the weaver and potter to those of the modern manufacturer and designer-creators. Indian Designs Act, amended after India became member of TRIPS provides protection for the original/novel shape, configuration and ornamentation or pattern applied to an article by an industrial process judged solely by the eye.

Certain products are associated with the place of origin making its characteristics and quality dependant on the features of such source. Geographical indication identifies such manufacture in the territory of a country, where a given quality, reputation or other characteristics of such goods are essentially attributable to the product's geographical origin. Mysore Silk, Kanchepuram Saree, Mogha Saree of Assam, Darjeeling Tea, Champagne of France, Roquefort cheese are all examples of Geographical indication protection. There is an urgent need for educating people to identify GIs and protect the same under our legislation. Long way has to go in this aspect, as India has a widely differing geography, climate and culture, specific and or famous for unique product(s) ranging from Madurai Jasmine flower, Artistic metal works and paintings of Tanjore, Mangoes of Salem, Carved wooden statuettes of Orissa, Hyderabad pearls, Guntur Chilly, Tirunelveli Halwa, Dindugul Locks, Gangeyam Bull, Rajapalayam hunter dogs, Srivilliputur Milk peda, etc. pose unique problems to India. Protection of such tangible assets of India is itself a mammoth task as is evidenced from the protracted battles waged by India against USA in issues relating to Basmati Rice and Turmeric.

Intellectual Property regime has been expanded with the introduction of new types of Intellectual Properties. One such IP is found in the form of Plant Varieties. Plant Variety Protection and Farmers Rights Act, 2001 was passed by the Indian Government in the year 2001 to give effect to Article 27(3)(b) of Part II of TRIPS Agreement of WTO. TRIPS provided that the members shall either give patent protection or effective *sui generic* protection to the plant varieties. The Act gives an effective system for protection of rights of the breeders and farmers and encourages development of new varieties of plants. The Act follows the model of the International Union for Protection of New Varieties of Plants, 1991 with few deviations. The Act grants protection to New, Distinct, Uniform and Stable varieties of plants. It grants a variety of rights to plant breeders and farmers. Genetically modified plants can also get protection as plant varieties under this Act. The Act provides *sui generis* protection for agricultural biotechnology sector in India by granting exclusive rights to novel varieties of plants developed through sexual or asexual breeding or genetic modification. India has recognized the farmer's rights and community rights. It is unique in this feature.

India is rich in Biodiversity and Traditional knowledge/ Traditional Cultural Expressions. The importance of protecting our Traditional Knowledge from Biopiracy was realized by the State after the Turmeric, Neem and basmati rice issues that stirred public opinion. After consistent efforts, the Ministry of Science and Technology under the NISCAIR has created the Traditional Knowledge Digital Library [TKDL] wherein the formulations of Ayurveda, Siddha and unani have been collected from various texts and documented against Uniform Traditional Knowledge Resource Classification that is compatible with International Patent Classification. The TKDL acts as a link between the computer screen of the Patent examiner and the Traditional Knowledge prevalent in the country. The WIPO initiative for protection of Traditional knowledge and Traditional Cultural Expression is commendable and the *sui generic* model they have suggested is worth considering keeping in mind the local realities.

The 'glycolipids and other non-steroidal compounds with profound adaptogenic and immuno-enhancing properties' found in the fruits and leaves of "Arogyapaccha" herb known to Kani tribe people lead to implementation of 'benefit-sharing' system in Kerala for the first time. TBGRI [Tropical and Botanical Garden Research

Institute], which developed "jeevani" drug agreed to pay kani tribe's trust fifty percent of its profit to knowledge holders.

The Biodiversity Act was passed by the Indian Government in the year 2002 with an objective of conserving biodiversity, sustainable use of its components and fair and equitable sharing of benefits arising out of use of biological resources and associated knowledge. It was passed in compliance with Convention on Biodiversity, 1992. The Act not only ensures protection of biological resources in India by prohibiting bio-piracy and regulating bio-prospecting, but also ensures the sharing of benefits arising out of Intellectual Property relating to biological resources and affiliated knowledge of indigenous communities. It had set up a National Biodiversity Authority and State Biodiversity Boards to monitor the use and exploitation of biological resources. The National Biodiversity Authority plays a very important role in implementing the benefit sharing provisions of the Act, which mandated that all benefits arising out of Intellectual Property generated from knowledge of indigenous communities has to be shared with them. The Biodiversity Act incentivizes indigenous communities and research institutes to co-operate and develop traditional biological knowledge and resources.

In India, there is need for a separate law for the protection of Traditional Knowledge and Traditional Cultural Expression. Instead of defensive protection provided under the Patent Act, Plant Varieties legislation and the Biodiversity Act, a positive protection should be provided since the existing Intellectual Property regime is inadequate to protect the TK/TCE. Additionally, the pharma Industry should consider exploiting our rich traditional knowledge for developing new medicines and drugs for meeting the emerging global challenges.

The modernization of the Intellectual Property offices in India and the simplification of the procedures have made access to the IP Offices easier. To facilitate the speedy protection of the IP for new inventions and commercially valuable assets, WIPO has a cluster of treaties ensuring international registration or filing of applications thereby simplifying the application procedures and reduce the cost of such filing. The most important of these treaties are Patent

Cooperation Treaty 1970 the Madrid Agreement concerning the International Registration of Marks and Hague Agreement concerning the International depository of Industrial Designs.

The Patent Cooperation Treaty ensures legal effect of one single international patent application in all member states, gets information about potential patentability of the invention through the International Search Report and International Preliminary Examination Report and gets more time than what the inventor gets under the traditional patent system. The number of international application growing from 2,586 in 1979 to 1,35,602 in 2005 speaks volumes about the utilization of the international system by the innovators. Similarly the Madrid System allows registration of trade and service marks through a single international registration procedure.

Conclusion

There is a need for efficient machinery to enforce these rights. In this regard, WIPO has set up an advisory Committee on Enforcement of IPR which has initiated a new approach to enforcement. Members are to focus collectively on the real challenges that all states face in implementing practical procedures for enforcing rights while keeping the time and cost burden on administrative infrastructures to a minimum. At the domestic level, the MHRD has taken measures for sensitizing the authorities for enforcement of the copyrights. We realize that IP has become an empire in its own right. Universities that are involved in innovation and creativity must have a distinct IP policy as per the guidelines laid down by the UGC. The industries should integrate the IP practice in their Business plan and create a corporate culture that imbibes IP, as Intellectual capital is considered to be the most important assets of many of the world's larger companies. The IP system shall continue to serve the functions of stimulating inventive and innovative activity, encouraging development of new technology, commercialization of inventions, creations and every subject matter of IP and facilitation of technological information.

Intellectual Property Rights Demystified, 2008
Mu. Ramkumar & A. Jayakumar (ed.), pp. 129-139
New India Publishing Agency, New Delhi (India)
E-mail : newindiapublishingagency@gmail.com
Web: www.bookfactoryindia.com

12

Current and Future Trends of Intellectual Property Rights Management and Governance

R.SUBRAMANIYA BHARATHY
Periyar Institute of Management Studies (PRIMS), Periyar University, Salem – 636 011.

ABSTRACT

The concept and nature of intellectual property have undergone a paradigm shift during the last few decades. The importance of effective IPR governance has attracted the attention of its stakeholders. Hence, this paper focuses on the role of IPR governance and management practices for improving the quality of relationships among stakeholders besides documenting current and future trends of IPR governance and management.

INTELLECTUAL PROPERTY RIGHTS – AN INTRODUCTION

Intellectual property rights refer to the privileges granted by the government to any individual or organization for creative prowess. In recent years, such rights have gained immense importance. The laws in existence for protection and enforcement of these rights are meant to foster innovation and for regulating the use of inventions. These laws encompass five major types of intangible properties, namely, patents, designs, trademarks, copyrights and Geographic indications. It must be appreciated that intellectual property is so named because it shares the same characteristics associated with real and personal property, but is intangible unlike the latter. The term of protection in respect of these rights varies from country to country. In most countries, these rights are enforceable by civil proceedings.

Patent systems are rewarding mechanisms designed to encourage disclosure of information relating to inventions to the public. Exclusive rights are awarded for a fixed period of time in the country or countries where the patent rights have been awarded. However, under all patent systems, once this period has lapsed, anybody is free to use the invention in any manner. The benefits of an effective patents system are enormous. Investments in Research & Development in an organization can be recovered through effective patenting mechanisms. Further research is stimulated as competitors invent new alternatives and or better systems. The public also stand to gain, as inventions are required to be commercialized during the term of patent.

Designs are another form of intellectual property. Protection of designs are also important as a means of enabling the consumer to visualize and identify a product made by a specific manufacturer. Trade secrets, where a company keeps information secret, perhaps by enforcing a contract under which those given access to information are not permitted to disclose it to others.

Trademarks are primarily intended to indicate the source of goods and services. They also symbolize the quality of goods or services with which they are used. Most trademarks are words but they can be symbols and logos. Trademarks are distinctive names, phrases or marks used to identify products to consumers.

Copyrights protect the original work of an author finding expression in a tangible media. Such protection is automatically attained from the moment of creation and it prevents unauthorized use of the creation. Copyrights, which give the holder exclusive rights to control reproduction of works, such as books and music, for a certain period of time, extending beyond the lifetime of the author.

Organizations need to manage various forms of intellectual properties effectively. The concept of management of intellectual property rights in an organization covers the administration of all stages of management of an innovation from the original concept to the final commercialization of the invention and even beyond. It is therefore, a process that requires continual attention in any organization.

Countries that provide for protection of intellectual property benefit in many ways. They increase the general pool of information and knowledge. Adequate legal protection fosters investment and trade. When companies look for new markets or countries for new or expansion projects, countries with adequate intellectual property protection are preferred. It has come to be realized, specially in the current context, that it is important

- To understand the current Trends in IPR Governance,
- To anticipate the Future Trends in IPR Governance and
- To design strategies for managing and governing IPR in organizational context.

CURRENT TRENDS IN IPR GOVERNANCE AND MANAGEMENT

Recent trend in intellectual property law has been *EXPANSION:* that covers new types of subject matter such as databases, regulates new categories of activity in respect of the subject matter already protected, increases the duration of individual rights and removes restrictions and limitations on these rights. Another effect of this trend is *AN INCREASE IN THE TERM OF THE GOVERNMENT GRANTED RIGHTS* and an expansion of the definition of "author" to include corporations as the legitimate creators and owners of works. The concept of work for hire has had the effect of treating a corporation or business owner as the legal author of works created by people while employed.

Another trend is *INCREASE IN THE NUMBER AND TYPE OF WHAT IS CLAIMED AS INTELLECTUAL PROPERTY.* This has resulted in increasingly broad patents and trademarks: for instance, Microsoft attempting to trademark the phrase, "Where do you want to go today?". Trademarks in EU law can now encompass smells (e.g. of cut grass for tennis balls), shapes (e.g. of a soft drinks bottle), colors (e.g. red for fizzy drinks), words (e.g. COCA-COLA) and sounds (Intel, has registered four notes). The granting of patents for life forms, software algorithms and business models stretch the initial concept of giving the inventor limited rights to exclude the use of his/her invention. Some argue that these expansions harm an essential "bargain" driven between public and copyright holders. As most "new" ideas borrow from other ideas, it is thought that too many intellectual property laws will

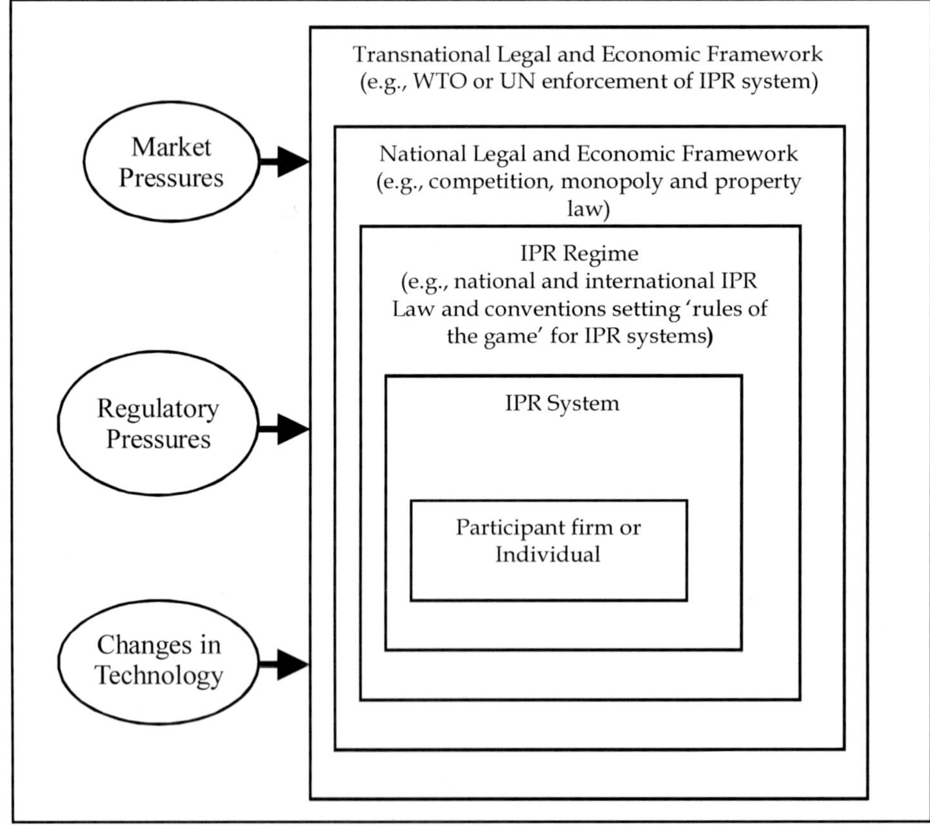

Scheme of IPR Governance

lead to a reduction of the overall creative output of a society. The expansion of exclusive rights is also alleged to have led to the emergence of organizations whose business model is to frivolously sue other companies.

The electronic age has seen *AN INCREASE IN THE ATTEMPT TO USE SOFTWARE BASED DIGITAL RIGHTS MANAGEMENT TOOLS* to restrict the copying and use of digital form of works. This can have the effect of limiting fair use provisions of copyright law. This would allow, in essence, creation of a book, which would disintegrate after one reading. As individuals have proven adept at circumventing such measures in the past, many copyright holders have also successfully lobbied for laws such as the Digital Millennium Copyright Act, which uses criminal law to prevent any circumvention of software used to enforce digital rights management systems. Equivalent provisions, to prevent circumvention of copyright protection existed in EU for some time, and are being expanded in, for example, Article 6 and 7 the Copyright Directive.

TRADE RELATED INTELLECTUAL PROPERTY RIGHTS

TRIPS require member states to provide strong IPR protection in many of these areas. For example,

- Copyright terms must extend to 50 years after the death of the author (although films and photographs are only required to have fixed 50 and 25 year terms, respectively).
- Copyright must be granted automatically and not based upon any "formality", such as registrations or systems of renewal.
- Computer programs must be regarded as "literary works" under copyright law and receive the same terms of protection.
- National exceptions to copyright (such as "fair use" in the United States) must be tightly constrained.
- Patents must be granted in all "fields of technology" regardless of public interest to do so.

- Exceptions to patent law must be limited almost as strictly as those to copyright law.
- In each state, intellectual property laws may not offer any benefits to local citizens, which are not available to citizens of other TRIPS signatories (this is called "national treatment"). TRIPS also has a most favored nation clause.

Since TRIPS was enacted, it has received a growing level of criticism from developing countries, academics and NGOs. But because of the rule-making processes in the WTO and the technical complexities of the laws in question, anything short of widespread and intense political opposition is unlikely to decrease the power of TRIPS.

Scheme of IPR Governance at the Macro Level

Form of Governance	**Dominant Stakeholder**	**Stakeholder Objectives**	**Role of IPR in Strategic Approaches**	**Expected Outcomes**
IPR Regime	Government	Investment, invention and innovation activities	IPR to stimulate economic incentives	Economic growth and social welfare
		Increased competition and market development	IPR to 'protect entrepreneurial talent'	Economic growth and social welfare
		Knowledge spillover	IPR to organize science, technology and creativity	Economic growth and social welfare
	IPR offices	Processing IPR applications. Granting and maintaining IPR	IPR sustain the importance of the IPR office	IPR generate income

Contd...

	IPR agents/IPR lawyers working in IPR offices and IPR agencies	Job, salaries and careers	IPR sustain the importance of the IPR agents/IPR lawyers working in IPR offices and IPR agencies	Maximize personal welfare
	Consumers	Maximize access to and minimize price on, products and services	Value from IPR regime is negative as it increases a cost on the production system and thereby increases price	Maximize personal welfare

POST-TRIPS EXPANSIONISM

Although the requirements of TRIPS are, from a policy perspective, extremely stringent, the lobby groups working to expand various IP laws have certainly found "limitations" in it. These have formed the basis for various bilateral and multilateral initiatives since the year 1994. The creation of anti-circumvention laws to protect digital restrictions management systems was achieved through the WIPO Copyright Treaty. The desire to further restrict the possibility of compulsory licenses for patents has led to provisions in recent bilateral US trade agreements. It is one thing for states to have intellectual property laws on their statues and another for governments to enforce them aggressively. This distinction has led to provisions in bilateral agreements, as well as proposals for WIPO and EU rules on Intellectual property enforcement.

KEY ASPECTS RELATED TO MANAGEMENT OF IPR

- The commercial potential of any research undertaken should be assessed. This is because, as already mentioned, it is essential to file an application for patent with at least provisional specification at the earliest, in order to establish priority for consideration of ownership and thus gain precedence over competitors.

IPR governance at the micro level

Form of governance	Dominant stakeholders	Stakeholder objective	Role of IPR approval in achievement of expected IPR outcomes
Sell and buy	Seller and Buyer	Short-term contractual market relationship	* Seller: Maximize income * Buyer: Access of ownership of productive knowledge, market power, venture capital, income from subsequent licensing agreements, or other.
License out and in	Licenser and licensee	Longer-term contractual market relationship	* Seller: Maximize income * Buyer: Access of ownership of productive knowledge, market power, venture capital, income from subsequent licensing agreements, or other.
Cross license	The forms engaging in a cr oss licensing agreement (All firms can be considered as both licensor and licenseee)	Longer-term non-exclusive contractual non-market relationship	* Licenser: Control on markets and maximize income from licensing agreements * Licensee: Access to a broader knowledge base.
IPR Roll	The firms engaging in an IPR pool (All firms can be considered as both licensor and license)	Longer-term non-exclusive contractual non-market relationship	* Increased access to productive knowledge on a royalty free bases * Cost cutting making the engaged firms price competitive. * Setting territories (i.e, market power) though exclusive cross-licensing agreements. * To enable an evolution or evolution of common standards.
External Firm license form IPR Pool	Licensor (the IPR pool) and licensee	Longer-term contractual market relationship	* Increased access to productive knowledge on a royalty free bases. * Cost cutting making the engaged firms price competitive. * To enable an evolution or evolution of common standards.

Contd...

Contd...

Share	The IPR share holders	Non-market share holding relationship	* Licenser: Control on markets and maximize income from licensing agreements * Licensee: Access to a broader knowledge base.
Any of the above	Lawyers, directly	Job, salaries	* The IPR which are shareholder-based can enter all shorts of IPR.

- All the scientists and technologists in the organization should be aware of the importance of various intellectual property issues and of the consequences to the organization of bad handling of the same.
- The patentability of the invention should be assessed carefully keeping in account all the considerations mentioned. There are two major aspects that need to be specifically looked into. The first one is the extent of prior art and prior public use. The second one is anticipating possibility of infringement of patent by others working in the same field and taking necessary steps to avoid the same. It should be understood that completing the procedure of patenting is both costly and time consuming and hence due considerations should be given to the potential advantages that could be accrued, before initiation of action for filing of patent.
- The time for filing the patent should be very carefully chosen. As mentioned earlier, the most ideal stage is when the idea is fully conceptualized. The invention can be properly protected only if the time for patenting is appropriately selected. Decisions relating to licensing of a patent or sale of a patent should be taken carefully depending upon several issues like the manufacturing and marketing strengths for that line of product which relates to the invention, potential commercial benefit through licensing *vis-a-vis* sale, etc. A systematic procedure for record maintenance should be in place. Complete record of all activities right from the conceptualization stage through the various stages is essential.
- Technological trends in the field of research undertaken should be continuously tracked. Regular patent information scan

should be undertaken. In respect of ownership of invention the employer-employee relationship should be clearly stated in a contract. There should be provision for sharing of benefits and for ensuring confidentiality of the know-how and technical information. Rights in respect of designs and trademarks should be wisely used to consolidate market positions.

- In the case of joint R&D collaborations between industry and or academic institutions or even international cooperation programs, the ownership of invention and the confidentiality aspects should be clearly stated in a contractual form right at the start of the collaboration. Aspects relating to sharing of know-how and data during the upscaling and commercialization stages of the invention between the various agencies concerned in a joint development should also be clearly specified.
- The process of licensing of technology and/or transfer of know-how should be very carefully managed. This would again depend upon several strategic considerations relating to both technology and commercial issues. While acquiring technology, the pros and cons or opting for licensing of patent or designs and drawings *vis-a-vis* transfer of know-now, are to be carefully assessed before decisions are taken.
- The research and development unit of a manufacturing organization should be given adequate focus and sufficient resources. Personnel involved in R&D should interact at all levels closely with the marketing, production and legal units of the organization. Only then, functions related to production of IPR can be properly coordinated as inputs required for the purpose can be efficiently accessed.
- One should at no stage lose sight of the various costs associated with the management of IPR. Especially, when dealing with foreign patents, it should be remembered that the process is very expensive. Hence, due consideration should be given to decisions regarding filing of patents outside the country.

- In primarily academic or research organizations, copyright issues gain precedence over patenting issues. However, it must be remembered that no information relating to potential inventions should be published, as it would be a bar to patenting.

Conclusion

With the recognition of the growing contribution of IPR policy to the performance of firms, sectors and nations, the role of IPR governance has become increasingly important. Countries that provide for protection of intellectual property benefit in many ways. Hence, effective governance and management of Intellectual Property Rights will do lot of good to not only to the Individual or Organization but also to the other stakeholders like government and the society.

References

Birgette Anderson and Sue Konzelmann., 2006 "Towards a useful theory of value creation from Intellectual Property Rights " ICFAI Jour. IPR, Vol.V No 1.

www.iprlawindia.org

Intellectual Property Rights Demystified, 2008
Mu. Ramkumar & A. Jayakumar (ed.), pp. 141-146
New India Publishing Agency, New Delhi (India)
E-mail : newindiapublishingagency@gmail.com
Web: www.bookfactoryindia.com

13

Protection of Biogeoresources

ANAMRAJU RAJANIKANTH
Birbal Sahni Institute of Palaeobotany, 53, University Road, Lucknow.

ABSTRACT

This paper is an attempt to draw the attention of readers of this volume to understand the importance of documentation and preservation of earth's resources.

INTRODUCTION

Earth has innumerable treasures that were and are being exploited by mankind. Geo-resources in the form of minerals, non-renewable hydrocarbons, paleontologic relics and related evidences indicate earth's evolutionary history. Continuum of biological activity albeit varying rates of proliferation had resulted in accumulation of natural resources embedded in Earth and distributed at specific geographical niches. Biological perspective of earth history is significant in unraveling bio-geo-sphere interactions through geological time. Fossil records of invertebrates, vertebrates and plants are signals of major changes in earth's evolutionary history. These constitute unparalleled windows to understand continental separation. Intercontinental and intra continental migration of living forms are also traced through fossil study. Research data on fossil material have become more relevant in the modern context and the data generated become tangible property as such. Since fossil hunters explore and extract fossil sites and bring the specimens to lab to study, the research material becomes movable property. They need to be conserved in museums/repositories/institutions, etc. Even the excavation sites should be carefully excavated and preserved for further understanding of earth's history.

As Earth's history is replete with cycles of similar events, documentation and preservation of such resources is important at least for the sake of understanding the future. Exceptionally preserved fossils often referred as *lagerstaetten* help in tracing the history of life and the distribution of continents (Briggs & Crowther 2003) and thus, such sites are conserved, akin to the way ancient civilization sites are preserved. This paper is an attempt to emphasize the need for conservation of such sites in India and their importance in the larger interests of understanding Earth's history as a whole.

INDIAN BIOGEORESOURCES

India has rich biogeoresources embedded in sedimentary sequences namely abundant fossil content. (Ayyasami, 2005). Some fossil sites in India are maintained by the Geological Survey of India, which include Saketi Fossil Park, Himachal Pradesh, known for rich mammalian fossils belonging to Siwalik sequences; Marine Gondwana Fossil Park at Mahendragarh, Sarguja district, Chattisgarh holds marine Permian fossils represented by pelecypods, lamellibranches, bryozoans, crinoids and forams; Akal Fossil Wood Park, Jaisalmer District, Rajasthan holds fossils of wood logs, leaves and gastropod shells of Jurassic period; National Fossil park at Tiruvakkarai, Villupuram District, Tamil Nadu holds huge wood logs, an excellent example of permineralized (Petrified) woods exemplifying sedimentary process itself (Tertiary Period) and Stromatolite Park, Jhamarkotra, Udaipur District, Rajasthan belong to Bhagwanpura Limestone of the Lower Vindhyan age. These indicate earliest life activities. Besides, India houses excellent sites of dinosaurian remains in the areas of town of Balasinor, Gujarat,in the sections near Narmada River from Jabalpur in Madhya Pradesh, Pranhita-Wardha Valley, (Maharashtra and Andhra Pradesh) and

Meghalaya. Many more potent areas in the Cauvery (Marine Cretaceous), Palar (Sriperumbudur), Krishna-Godavari (Raghavapuram, Ommevaram), Gondwana deposits of Son-Mahanadi, Damodar, Sourashtra (Vastan), Jharkhand (Rajmahal), Deccan Intertrappean sequences (Maharashtra, Andhra Pradesh, Madhya Pradesh) and Himalayan Zone require special care to protect palaeontologic and geologic wealth particularly coal and lignite deposits.

In order to perpetuate challenging areas of research in earth sciences, it is essential to preserve the legacy of geo-resources for the posterity (Radhakrishna 2003, Tandon & Gupta 1990) and conservatory mechanism to accomplish different end goals of chosen spheres of knowledge (Prasad 2006).

IPR AND EARTH RESOURCES

Modern IPR milieu emphasizes conferring rights over intangible creations of human intellect. It is related to pieces of information that can be incorporated in tangible objects. Intellectual Property is the information as such which is protected. New techniques to preserve and extracting valuable information from the past relics itself is an exciting branch of study and geoscientists have a greater responsibility to become relevant in changing times. Fortunately Indian culture is based on sharing of knowledge and not commercialization of knowledge. Since scientists too are social outputs, there is an added advantage of mutual sharing. In this context, protecting our geo-bio heritage bear far reaching benefits to society as such. In this pursuit, efforts in the following directions may help to concretize resource safeguarding.

Government, National Institutions, Museums and Research laboratories should look after fossil localities. Unfortunately, India lags behind in implementing geo-related laws. Potential geological sites should be brought under one umbrella. A co-operative venture by earth related organizations is essential. Sites bearing stratigraphic sections, units showing exceptional diversity of fossils-both fauna and flora should be recognized and protected. International Union for Conservation of Nature and Natural resources (IUCN) has a great role to play to protect geological sites. The world heritage geological working group should intensify its efforts in identifying internationally significant sites. The Indian geoscientists bear a dismal record of not making some of the excellent Indian geo-sites declared under World Heritage listing. The newly formed Ministry of Earth Sciences has a major role in taking initiatives to protect geo-resources NGO's and other geo-organizations/Associations/clubs should conduct awareness programs to conserve phyto-geo- resources. Protected zones may be identified for better coordination.

WHAT IS TO BE DONE FOR PRESERVATION OF BIOGEORESOURCES ?

Data on georesources should be compiled consisting of the following information.

- Geographical location, physical features, altitude, climate, vegetation
- Conservation value, Resource Reserve potential, Management plan for important geological sites, Aesthetic value and Geo-tourism prospect.

This exercise is needed to educate the concerned authorities to initiate appropriate steps to protect prospective sites. In addition, the following have to be attempted.

- Geo-resource parks have to be notified in the way wildlife sanctuaries and National parks are notified and protected.
- An inventory of valuable sites should be prepared.
- Natures' (EARTH) contribution to human development should be widely propagated.
- Internationally important geo-resource sites including those present in India be brought under World heritage list.
- Systematic and strategic approach to prepare books, handouts, etc. and distribution to wide range of people for enhancing wider participation in saving georesources.
- Policing and surveillance as part of an integrated management plan.

- Initiation of sustainable plans through coordinated approach.
- Transmission of information to future generations.

REMARKS

Plundering of geo-resource by modern man leads to ecosystem changes and habitat destruction to many bio-forms. There is a dire necessity of having a strict legislature to thwart any disrespect to nature. Many instances of uncontrolled mining, misuse of sedimentary units with fossil-resource, indifference to create geo-tourist parks, reluctance to declare prosperous geo-sites as heritage zones is a matter of concern. It is high time we look into protection and conservation of valuable paleontological and geological material to preserve earth's legacy (Prasad, 2006; Nagendra, 2004; Sahni, 2005).

The International Union of History and Philosophy of Science has been active to preserve archives and the International Commission on the History of Geological Sciences too has been contributing to such venture. There is an increasing concern to conserve geo-heritage since lot of damage has been done in the name of development and even religion due to which much of rock resource with valuable minerals are being lost (Radhakrishna, 2005, Mathur 2005, Khanna 2005, Barthwal 2006). Information regarding important geo-bio sites have been compiled in the form of books and guides which have to be distributed among educational institutions and responsible local bodies to make them aware of importance of bioresources. The Geological Survey of India has brought out a publication on National Geological Monuments and Birbal Sahni institute Lucknow has published a series of Catalogues on fossil holotype, localities, horizon and age etc. (*www.bsip.res.in).*

References

Ayyasami, K., 2005 Palaeontology, A multiple science. Diamond Jubilee National Conference, BSIP, Abst.:4

Barthwal, B., 2006 Conservation of Geological Heritage. Jour.Geol.Soc. v. 67.pp.132-133.

Briggs, D.E.G. and Crowther, P.R., 2003.Palaeobiology II Blackwell Publishing. 583p.

Lipps, J.H., 2006 Abstracts, Symposium on the palaeontological parks- The world wide conservation of outstanding fossil sites, II Inter.Palaeont.Congress. Beijing.

Khanna, V.K., 2005 Preserve the natural geological museums Jour.Geol.Soc. v.66. pp.521.

Mathur, S.M., 2005 Vandalism in the name of religion. Jour.Geol.Soc.Ind. v.66. pp.521.

Mehrotra, N.C., Venkatachala, B.S. and Kapoor, P.N., 2005. Palynology in Hydrocarbon Exploration: The Indian scenario, Part II- Spatial and Temporal distribution of significant Spores, Pollen and Dinoflagellate Cysts in the Mesozoic-Cenozoic sediments of Petroliferous Basins. Geol. Soc. India Memoir. v.61. pp.1-128.

Prasad, G.V.R., 2006 Palaeontological researches in India –Future directions, BSS, Jammu University, pp. 1-56.

Radhakrishna,B.P., 2003 Random Harvest Geol.Soc.Ind.Mem. v.51. pp.272-277.

Radhakrishna, B.P., 2005 Vandalism in the name of religion Jour.Geol.Soc.Ind. v.66. pp.137-140.

Nagendra, R., 2004 Cretaceous out crop sequence stratigraphy of Tiruchirapalli, India. Jour.Geol.Soc.Ind. v. 65. pp.1-62.

Sahni, A., 2005 Paleobiology: disintegration of an integrated Science, Diamond Jubilee National Conference, BSIP, Abst: 114.

Sahni, A., 2006 Temporal constraints and depositional palaeoenvironments of the Vastan Lignite sequence Gujarat: Analogy for the Cambay Shale Hydrocarbon Source Rock Indian Jour.Petroleum Geology 15(1) pp.1-20.

Intellectual Property Rights Demystified, 2008
Mu. Ramkumar & A. Jayakumar (ed.), pp. 147-150
New India Publishing Agency, New Delhi (India)
E-mail : newindiapublishingagency@gmail.com
Web: www.bookfactoryindia.com

14

Suggested Course of Action for Familiarization of IPR

***Mu.RAMKUMAR, +A.JAYAKUMAR, *K.ANBARASU, *R.SURESH and #T.POONGODI VIJAYAKUMAR**
*Department of Geology, +Department of Commerce, #Department of Food Science, Periyar University, Salem – 636 011.

ABSTRACT

This paper presents few measures to be taken up by academic institutions, professional societies, industrial bodies and governmental agencies for the propagation of information of IPR in terms of encouragement of publication of books on IPR, establishment of IPR cells in academic and professional institutions and making IPR education as part of curriculum in Universities and institutions of higher learning.

INTRODUCTION

A national workshop sponsored by Council of Scientific and Industrial Consultancy, New Delhi and Tamil Nadu State Council for Science and Technology was conducted at the Periyar University, Salem, Tamil Nadu. The workshop was mainly intended for enlightening the geoscientists from academic, governmental and industrial sectors on IPR. However, owing to the demand from different walks namely, teachers and research scholars of science fields and professional geologists, the workshop turned out to be meant for all those interested in IPR. This paper is the result of observations made by the authors prior to, during and after the workshop. It is believed that enactment of the measures listed herein would result not only in increased awareness on IPR among the innovators, but also would benefit our country in the long run.

SUGGESTIONS FOR FAMILIARIZATION OF IPR

It is a known fact that awareness on IPR among scientific community is dismal when compared with the enlightenment existing among professionals and academics of IT and pharma fields. To eradicate such ignorance, periodic Workshops on IPR issues should be conducted. The national laboratories, universities and other scientific organizations should make special training on IPR compulsory for professional scientists, researchers and teachers. Thus, this enlightenment would bring not only improved economic development for our country, but also inculcate ethical practice in acknowledging IP of coworkers.

In accordance with the conventions of Human Rights Bodies of International Arena and the treaties signed by the Government of India in protection of Human Rights, the University Grants Commission (UGC) has directed all the Universities of India to impart education on Human Rights and made it as a compulsory paper in order to make the students familiar with Human Rights. IPR education should also be introduced in the University curriculum along similar lines and in this regard, any action by UGG would be welcomed by one and all.

Although volumes are written on the conventions/treaties and on the importance of IPR and its protection, non-availability of IPR information in the form of a ready reckoner on IPR/patents/designs/ copyright and laws, application forms and procedures thwarts common-man to understand IPR and related issues. Enhanced awareness on IPR laws and copyright procedures would help filings for IPR by scientists, teachers and researchers. (*Authors of papers included in this volume feel that publication of this volume and making wide circulation of it would address the issue*).

It is felt that ignorance on legal procedures in filing for IPR and reluctance of scientists and researchers to approach appropriate authorities for claiming copyright are the two major issues. Addressing these two issues would increase the number of patent and copyright filings. Hence, it is recommended that a specific agency/chair/authority has to be established in each university jurisdiction. Prime function of such agency/chair/authority should be to identify patentable results/inventions emanating from research works by scientists/academicians/professionals and facilitate filing for patents/copyrights. To begin with, enlisting the services of locally available legal attorney specializing on IPR in every University Jurisdiction area would be of help.

Conclusion

The workshop on GEO-IPR'2006 has highlighted the dismal knowledge on IPR among researchers and academics and the need for enlightening them through employing various media and training programs. These two tasks are to be implemented immediately on a large scale owing to the fact that in the current global economic scenario and the transformation of India from agrarian economy to knowledge, technology and services based economy, adherence to the global practices of preservation and utilization of knowledgebase is essential in order to make India not only a self reliant nation, but also to a strong leader in supply of cutting edge technology to developed and less developed nations, which would be the chief driver of economic growth in the near future.

While the publication of this volume and wide distribution of it would serve the purpose of making available IPR information at a single location, conductance of workshops and training programs should be with the following objectives.

a. To sensitize the scientists on the vistas of protecting scientific knowledge and processes for the benefit of our country's wealth and economic development.

b. To spread knowledge on IPR regime, laws and procedures in filing for patents among scientists and researchers and to train the scientists and researchers to become information disseminators on IPR and act as facilitators for patent filing.

It is believed that adherence to these would help create higher levels of awareness among all those concerned paving way for our country's rapid strides in the transformation of agrarian economy to knowledge based economy.

15

Annexure

FORM 1

FEE Rs. 1000

Application for registration of designs.
section 5 and 44

You are requested to register the accompanying in

[1]Insert number of class — Class No.[1]…………………… in ……………...….......

[2]Insert (in full) the name address and nationality — the name of [2] ……………………………………………………………………………

……………………………………………………………………………

……………………………………………………………………………

...……………………… who claim(s) to be the proprietor(s) thereof.

[3]State whether drawings, photographs, tracings or specimens. — Four exactly similar[3] ………………………………of the design accompany this request.

[4]Insert name of article or articles to which the design is to be applied or state trade description of each of the articles contained in the set — The design is to be applied to[4] ……………………….............

……………………………………………………………………………

……………………………………………………………………………

……………………………………………………………………………

[5]Strike out these words if previous registration has been effected. — [5]The design has been previously registered in Class(es). ….............…………………….. Under No.

Details of first application in UK or convention country or group of countries or inter-governmental organisation.

(i) Name of country.

(i) Official date.

(ii) Official number.

[6]Unless an address for service in India in given, the request may not be considered. — Address for service[6] in India is -

……………………………………………………………….....

………………………………………………………….......

Declaration:

The applicant claims to be the proprietors of the design and that to the best of his knowledge and belief the design is new or original.

Dated this …….………. Day of …….…….19

[7]To be signed by the applicant or by authorised agent. — (Signed)[7]……………………………………………....

TO
THE CONTROLLER OF DESIGNS,
THE PATENT OFFICE, CALCUTTA.

* Strike out the words if no previous registration or priority claim has been effected

FORM 2

Fee Rs. 500

CLAIM UNDER SECTION 8(1) TO PROCEED AS AN APPLICANT OR JOINT APPLICANT

I (or We)[1] ____________________

____

hereby request that the application for Design no. __________ of __________ dated __________ made by[2] ____________________

____

____________________ may proceed in the name(s) of[3] __________

I/we claim to be entitled to proceed as applicant(s) for the Design virtue of[4]

____

____

____

And in the proof whether I/We transmit the accompanying[5] ____________________

My/Our address for service in India is :-

____

____

Dated this __________ day of __________ 19

Signature[6]

____

I/We[7] ____________________ consent to the above request.

(Signature)[8] ____________________

TO
THE CONTROLLER OF DESIGNS,
THE PATENT OFFICE, CALCUTTA.

[1] State name, address and nationality of claimants.

[2] State the name of the applicant(s) for Design.

[3] Insert (in full) name, address and nationality of the person(s) in whose name(s) it is requested that the application shall proceed.

[4] Give particulars of such document giving its date, the parties there of and showing how the claim here made is substantiated.

[5] State the nature of the document (copy).

[6] To be signed by the claimant(s).

[7] State name address and nationality of the applicant.

[8] To be signed by applicant(s) or authorised agent.

Note: Strick out which ever is inapplicable

FORM 3

FEE Rs. 2000

APPLICATION TO EXTEND COPYRIGHT.

Section 11

[1] Insert number of design.

[2] Insert Class.

[3] To be signed by the applicant or authorised agent.

You are requested by the undersigned who is/are the registered proprietor(s) of the Design No.[1] ________________ registered in Class[2] __________________ to extend the period of copyright for a period of five years.

Adderss for service in India is :-

____

____

Dated this _______________ day of ________________ 2000

(Signed)[3] ____

TO
THE CONTROLLER OF DESIGNS
THE PATENT OFFICE, CALCUTTA.

FORM 4

FEE Rs. 1000

APPLICATION FOR THE RESTORATION OF DESIGN UNDER SECTION 12(2)

[See rule 24]

[1] Insert the name (in full), address and nationality of applicant(s).

[2] State the last date when fee was due.

[3] To be signed by the applicant(s) or if the applicant(s) is/are absent from India, by authorised agent.

I (or/we)[1] ______________________

Hereby apply for an order of the Controller for the restoration of Design No. ____________

____________ of ____________

dated ____________ granted to ____________

____

The circumstance which led to the failure to pay the extension fee of Rs. ____________ on or before the[2] ____________ day of ____________ are as follows :-

____

____

I/we declare that I/We have not assigned the Design to any other person(s) and that the fact and matters stated herein are true to the best of my/our knowledge, information and belief.

My/our address for service in India is :-

____

____

Dated this ____________ day of ____________ 19

(Signature)[3] ....

TO
THE CONTROLLER OF DESIGNS,
THE PATENT OFFICE, CALCUTTA.

Note : Strike out whichever is inapplicable.

THE GEOGRAPHICAL INDICATIONS OF GOODS
(REGISTRATION & PROTECTION) ACT, 1999

(To be filed in triplicate alongwith the Statement of Case accompanied by five additional representation of the geographical indication)

One representation to be fixed within the space and five others to be send separately

FORM GI-1

A	**Application for the registration of a geographical indication in Part A of the Register** Section 11(1), Rule 23(2) Fee: Rs. 5,000 (See entry No.1A of the First Schedule)	
B	**Application for the registration of a geographical indication in Part A of the Register from a convention country** Section 11(1), 84(1), rule 23(3) Fee: Rs. 5,000 (See entry No.1Bof the First Schedule)	

1. Application is hereby made by (a) ______________ for the registration in Part A of the Register of the accompanying geographical indication furnishing the following particulars:
   - Name of the Applicant:
   - Address:
   - List of association of persons/producers/organisation/authority:
   - Type of goods:
   - Specification:
   - Name of the geographical indication[and particulars]:
   - Description of the goods:
   - Geographical area of production and map:
   - Proof of origin[Historical records]
   - Method of Production:
   - Uniqueness:
   - Inspection Body:
   - Other:

   Along with the Statement of Case in Class (b)__________ (b)_______in respect of (c)______________in the name(s) of (d)__________ whose address is (e)______________________________ who claims to represent the interest of the producers of the said goods to which the geographical indication relates and which is in continuous use since __________in respect of the said goods.

2. The application shall include such other particulars called for in rule 32(1) in the Statement of Case
3. All communications relating to this application may be sent to the following address in India:
4. In the case of an application from a convention country the following additional particulars shall also be furnished

a) Designation of the country of origin of the geographical indication
b) Evidence as to the existing protection of the geographical indication in its country of origin, such as the title and the date of the relevant legislative or administrative provisions, the judicial decisions or the date and number of the registration, and copies, of such documentation

(5)SIGNATURE

NAME OF THE SIGNATORY
(IN BLOCK LETTERS)

C	**A single application for the registration of a geographical indication in Part A of the Register for goods falling in different classes** Section 11(3), rule 23(5) Fee: Rs. 5,000 for each class (See entry No.1C of the First Schedule)	
D	**A single application for the registration of a geographical indication in Part A of the Register for goods falling in different classes from a convention country** Section 11(3), rule 23(4) Fee: Rs. 5,000 for each class (See entry No.1D of the First Schedule)	

1. **1.** Application is hereby made by (a) _______________ for the registration in Part A of the Register of the accompanying geographical indication furnishing the following particulars:
   - Name of the Applicant:
   - Address:
   - List of association of persons/producers/organisation/authority:
   - Type of goods:
   - Specification:
   - Name of the geographical indication[and particulars]:
   - Description of the goods:
   - Geographical area of production and map:
   - Proof of origin[historical records]
   - Method of Production:
   - Uniqueness:
   - Inspection Body:
   - Other:

along with the Statement of Case in Class
(i) class a .... in respect of b ....
(ii) class a .... in respect of b ....
(iii) class a .... in respect of b ....
in the name(s) of c.................. whose address is(d) .... who claim (s) to represent the interest of the producers of the goods to which the geographical indication relates and which geographical indication is used continuously since .... in respect of the said goods.

2. The application shall include such other particulars called for in rule 32(1) in the Statement of Case
3. All communications relating to this application may be sent to the following address in India:
4. In the case of an application from a convention country the following additional particulars shall also be furnished

a) Designation of the country of origin of the geographical indication
b) Evidence as to the existing protection of the geographical indication in its country of origin, such as the title and the date of the relevant legislative or administrative provisions, the judicial decisions or the date and number of the registration, and copies, of such documentation

(5)SIGNATURE

NAME OF THE SIGNATORY
(IN BLOCK LETTERS)

For instruction please see overleaf

GI-1A to 1D

The Registrar of Geographical Indications,
The office of Geographical Indications Registry.

a). Strike out whichever is not applicable.
b). The Registrars' direction may be obtained if the class of the goods is not known.
c). Here specify the goods. Only goods included in one and the same class to be specified.
d). Insert legibly the full name, description (occupation and calling and nationality of the applicant). In the case of a body corporate or firm the country of incorporation or the names and descriptions of the partners composing the firm and the nature of registration, if any, as the case may be, should be stated. See rule 15.
e) Signature of the applicant or his agent

FORM 1 THE PATENTS ACT 1970 (39 of 1970) & The Patents Rules, 2003 APPLICATION FOR GRANT OF PATENT **(See section 7,54&135and rule20 (1))**	(FOR OFFICE USE ONLY) Application No: Filing Date: Amount of Fee Paid: CBR No: Signature:

1. APPLICANT (S)

Name	Nationality	Address

2. INVENTOR (S)

Name	Nationality	Address

3. TITLE OF THE INVENTION

4. ADDRESS FOR CORRESPONDENCE OF APPLICANT/AUTHORIZED PATENT AGENT IN INDIA	Telephone No. Fax No. Mobile No. E-mail:

5. PRIORITY PARTICULARS OF THE APPLICATION (S) FILED IN CONVENTION COUNTRY

Country	Application Number	Filing Date	Name of the Applicant	Title of the Invention

6. PARTICULARS FOR FILING PATENT COOPERATION TREATY (PCT) NATIONAL PHASE APPLICATION

International application number.	International filing date as allotted by the receiving office.

7. PARTICULARS FOR FILING DIVISIONAL APPLICATION

Original (first) application number.	Date of filing of Original (first) application

8. PARTICULARS FOR FILING PATENT OF ADDITION

Main application/patent Number.	Date of filing of main application

9. DECLARATIONS:

(i) Declaration by the inventor(s)

I/We, the above named inventor(s) is/are the true & first inventor(s) for this invention and declare that the applicant(s)herein is/are my/our assignee or legal representative.

(a) Date_________
(b) Signature(s)
(c) Name(s)

(ii) Declaration by the applicant(s) in the convention country

I/We, the applicant(s) in the convention country declare that the applicant(s)herein is/are my/our assignee or legal representative.

(a) Date_________
(b) Signature(s)
(c) Name(s) of the signatory

(iii) Declaration by the applicant(s):
I/We, the applicant(s) hereby declare(s) that: -

- ❑ I am /We are in possession of the above-mentioned invention
- ❑ The provisional/complete specification relating to the invention is filed with this application.
- ❑ The invention as disclosed in the specification uses the biological material from India and the necessary permission from the competent authority shall be submitted by me/us before the grant of patent to me/us.
- ❑ There is no lawful ground of objection to the grant of the Patent to me/us.
- ❑ I am/ We are the assignee or legal representative of true & first inventors.
- ❑ The application or each of the applications, particulars of which are given in Para -5 was the first application in convention country/countries in respect of my/our invention.
- ❑ I/We claim the priority from the above mentioned application(s) filed in convention country/countries and state that no application for protection in respect of the invention had been made in a convention country before that date by me/us or by any person from which I/We derive the title.
- ❑ My/our application in India is based on international application under Patent Cooperation Treaty (PCT) as mentioned in Para - 6.
- ❑ The application is divided out of my/our application particulars of which are given in Para - 7 and pray that this application may be treated as deemed to have been filed on ________ under sec.16 of the Act.
- ❑ The said invention is an improvement in or modification of the invention particulars of which are given in Para - 8.

10. Following are the attachments with the application:

(a) Provisional specification/Complete specification
(b) Complete specification (in conformation with the international application)/as amended before the International Preliminary Examination Authority (IPEA), as applicable (2 copies), No. of pages _____ No. of claims_________
(c) Drawings (in conformation with the international application)/as amended before the International Preliminary Examination Authority (IPEA), as applicable (2 copies),No. of sheets__________
(d) Priority documents
(e) Translation of priority document/Specification/International Search Report
(f) Statement and undertaking on Form 3
(g) Power of Authority
(h) Declaration of inventorship on Form5
(i) Sequence listing in electronic form
(j) ....

Fee Rs............... ....in Cash./ Cheque / Bank Draft bearing no.........................
Date..........................on ....Bank.

I/We hereby declare that to the best of my/our knowledge, information and belief the fact and matters stated herein are correct and I/We request that a patent may be granted to me/us for the said invention.

Dated this ....day of.................20...........

Signature:-
Name:

Note: -*Repeat boxes in case of more than one entry.
***To be signed by the applicant(s) or by authorized registered patent agent otherwise where mentioned.**
***Tick (√)/cross (×) whichever is applicable/not applicable in declaration in para-9.**
***Name of the inventor and applicant should be given in full, family name in the beginning.**
***Complete address of the inventor and applicant should be given stating the postal index no./code, state and country. *Strike out the column which is/are not applicable** * For fee: See First Schedule

<table>
<tr><td colspan="2" align="center">FORM 2
THE PATENT ACT 1970
(39 of 1970)
&
The Patents Rules, 2003
PROVISIONAL/COMPLETE SPECIFICATION
(See section 10 and rule13)</td></tr>
<tr><td colspan="2">1. TITLE OF THE INVENTION</td></tr>
<tr><td colspan="2">2. APPLICANT (S)
(a) NAME
(b) NATIONALITY
(c) ADDRESS</td></tr>
<tr><td colspan="2">3. PREAMBLE TO THE DESCRIPTION</td></tr>
<tr><td>PROVISIONAL

The following specification describes the invention.</td><td>COMPLETE

The following specification particularly describes the invention and the manner in which it is to be performed.</td></tr>
<tr><td colspan="2">4. DESCRIPTION (Description shall start from next page.)</td></tr>
<tr><td colspan="2">5. CLAIMS (not applicable for provisional specification. Claims should start with the preamble —“I/we claim” on separate page)</td></tr>
<tr><td colspan="2">6. DATE AND SIGNATURE (to be given at the end of last page of specification)</td></tr>
<tr><td colspan="2">7. ABSTRACT OF THE INVENTION (to be given along with complete specification on separate page)</td></tr>
<tr><td colspan="2">Note: -
*Repeat boxes in case of more than one entry.
*To be signed by the applicant(s) or by authorized registered patent agent.
*Name of the applicant should be given in full , family name in the beginning .
*Complete address of the applicant should be given stating the postal index no./code, state and country.
*Strike out the column which is/are not applicable</td></tr>
</table>

FORM 3

THE PATENTS ACT, 1970
(39 of 1970)
&
The Patents Rules, 2003

STATEMENT AND UNDERTAKING UNDER SECTION 8
(See section 8, rule 12)

1. Namely of the applicant(s). I/We.[1]..______________________________

____

hereby declare:

2. Name, address and nationality of the joint applicant: (i) that I/We have not made any application for the same/substantially the same invention outside India.

Or

(ii) that I/We who have made this application No.________________ Dated______ alone/jointly with [2]..., made for the same/substantially same invention, application(s) for patent in the other countries, the particulars of which are given below:

Name of the country.	Date of application	Application No.	Status of the application	Date of publication	Date of grant

3. Name and address of the assignee (iii) that the rights in the application(s) has/have been assigned to. [3].

____

that I/We undertake that upto the date of grant of the patent, by the Controller, I/We would keep him informed in writing the details regarding corresponding applications for patents filed outside India within three months from the date of filing of such application.

Dated this .... day of 20

4. To be signed by the applicant or his authorised registered patent agent.

Signature[4]..

5. Name of the natural person who has signed. ( )[5]

To
The Controller of Patents,
The Patent Office, At

Note: Strike out whichever is not applicable.

FORM 4

THE PATENTS ACT, 1970
(39 of 1970)
&
The Patents Rules, 2003

REQUEST FOR EXTENSION OF TIME
[See sections 53(2) and 142(4)
rules 13(6), 24B(4)(ii), 80(1A) and 130]

1. Name of the applicant.	I/We.[1] ________________________________ ____ ____ hereby request for extension of time for __________ month(s) under Section/Rule ______________ in connection with my / our application / Patent No.__________ The reasons for making the request are as follows: - Dated this .... day of 20
2. To be signed by the applicant or his authorised registered patent agent.	Signature [2] (--) [3]
3. Name of the natural person who has signed	
	To The Controller of Patents, The Patent Office, At ....

Note: For fee : See First Schedule.

FORM 5
THE PATENTS ACT, 1970
(39 of 1970)

&

The Patents Rules, 2003

DECLARATION AS TO INVENTORSHIP

[See section 10(6) and rule 13(6)]

1. NAME OF APPLICANT (S)	

hereby declare that the true and first inventor(s) of the invention disclosed in the complete specification filed in pursuance of my /our application numbered dated is/are

2. INVENTOR (S)

(a) NAME
(b) NATIONALITY
(c) ADDRESS

Dated this ....day of.................20............

Signature: -
Name of the signatory: -

3. DECLARATION TO BE GIVEN WHEN THE APPLICATION IN INDIA IS FILED BY THE APPLICANT (S) IN THE CONVENTION COUNTRY: -

We the applicant(s) in the convention country hereby declare that our right to apply for a patent in India is by way of assignment from the true and first inventor(s).

Dated this ....day of..................20............

Signature: -
Name of the signatory: -

4. STATEMENT (to be signed by the additional inventor(s) not mentioned in the application form)

I/We assent to the invention referred to in the above declaration, being included in the complete specification filed in pursuance of the stated application.

Dated this ....day of..................20............

Signature of the additional inventor(s): -

Name: -

Note

***Repeat boxes in case of more than one entry.**

***To be signed by the applicant(s) or by authorized registered patent agent otherwise where mentioned.**

***Name of the inventor and applicant should be given in full, family name in the beginning .**

***Complete address of the inventor should be given stating the postal index no./code, state and country.**

***Strike out the column which is/ are not applicable**

FORM 6

THE PATENTS ACT, 1970
(39 of 1970)
&
The Patents Rules, 2003

CLAIM OR REQUEST REGARDING ANY CHANGE IN APPLICANT FOR PATENT

[See sections 20(1), 20(4) and 20(5); rules 34(1), 35(1) and 36(1)]

I/We,[1] ____________________
(a) [2] ____________________
(b) [3] ____________________
(c) [4] ____________________

hereby request that the application for patent No. .... dated .... made by[5]. ____________________
____
may proceed in my/our name and further request that direction of the Controller, if necessary be made in that effect
Reasons for making the above request are as follows:-
____
____

I furnish the following document(s) in support of my above request:[6]
(a)[7] ____________
(b)[7] ____________
(c)[7] ____________

My/our address for service in India is:.[8]
____
____

1. Repeat the columns (a) to (c) if there are more than one applicant.
2. Insert the name in full. The family or principal name in the beginning if the applicant is a natural person.
3. Insert the complete address including postal index number/code and state and/or country.
4. Insert the nationality.
5. State the name of the applicant(s) for patent.
6. Original and certified copies of the documents shall accompany the claim or request. Consent by the legal representative of the deceased joint applicant shall be filed whenever required.
7. Insert the details of the documents.
8. Complete address including postal index number/code and state along with Telephone and fax number(s).
9. To be signed by the applicant (s) or authorized registered patent agent.
10. Name of the natural person who has signed.

Dated this .... day of ...., 200

Signature [9] ..

(--) [10].

To
The Controller of Patents,
The Patent Office,
At ....

N.B.: This form is not applicable for mere change of name.
Note: (a) Strike out whichever is not applicable.
(b) For fee:-See First Schedule.

FORM 7

THE PATENTS ACT, 1970
(39 of 1970)
&
The Patents Rules, 2003

NOTICE OF OPPOSITION
[See sections 25(3) and rule 55A]

1. State names, address and nationality.	I/We,[1]... ____ ____ ____
2. State the grounds taken one after another.	hereby give notice of opposition to patent No. ....) granted on application No. ....dated............... published on dated...............made by____
3. Complete address including postal index number/code and state along with Telephone and fax number.	on the grounds [2]. ____ ____
4. To be signed by the opponent or by his authorized registered patent agent.	My/Our address for services in India is..[3] ....
5. Name of the natural person who has signed.	Signature -[4].... (--) [5]....

To
The Controller of Patents,
The Patent Office,
At ....

For fee : See First Schedule.

FORM TM-1

THE TRADE MARKS ACT, 1999

Agent's code No:

Proprietor's code No:

Fee: Rs.2500/

Application for registration of a trade mark for goods or services (other than a collective mark or a certification trade mark)in the register section 18(1), 25(2).

(To be filed in triplicate accompanied by five additional representations of the trade mark)

One representation to be fixed within this space and five others to be sent separately.

Representation of a larger size may be folded but must then be mounted upon linen or other su

itable material and affixed hereto. (See rule 28).

Application is hereby made for registration in the register of the accompanying

trade mark in class [1] .... in respect of [2] ....in the name(s) of

[3].................. whose address is [4] .... who claim (s) to be the proprietor(s) thereof [and by whom the said mark is proposed to be used [5] or (and by whom and his (their) predecessor(s) in title [6] the said mark has been continuously used since ....] in respect of the said goods or services.7

8.................................. [9] ....

All communications relating to this application may be sent to the following address in India:-

Dated this ....day of ....20............

[10]..SIGNATURE

NAME OF SIGNATORY IN LETTERS.

To

The Registrar of Trade marks,

The office of the Trade Marks Registry at.(11)......................

1. The Registrar's direction may be obtained if the class of the goods or services is not known.
2. Specify the goods or services for the class in respect of which application is made. A separate sheet detailing the goods or services may be used. The specification of goods or services should not ordinarily exceed five hundred characters. An excess space fee of Rs.10 per character is payable beyond this limit. See rule 25(16) The applicant shall state the exact number of excess characters where the specification of goods or services exceeds of five hundred characters at the space provided immediately before the signature.
3. Insert legibly the full name, description (occupation, calling and nationality of the applicant). In the case of a body corporate or firm the country of incorporation or the names and descriptions of the partners composing the firm and the nature of registration, if any, as the case may be, should be stated. (See rule 16).
4. The applicant shall state the address of his principal place of business in India. if any. (See rules 3 and 17) If the applicant carries on business in the goods or services for which registration is sought at only one place in India such fact should be stated and the address of the place given. If the applicant carries on business in the goods or services concerned at more places than one in India the applicant should state such fact and give the address of that place of business which he considers to be his principal place of business. If, however, the applicant does not carry on business in the goods or services concerned but carries on business in other goods or services at any one place in India this fact should be stated and the address of that place given; and where the applicant carries on such business at more places than one in India such fact should be stated and the address of the place which he considers to be his principal place of business given. Where the applicant is not carrying on any business in India the fact should be stated and the place of his residence in India, if any, should be stated and the address of that place given. In addition to the principal place of business or of residence in India, as the case may be, an applicant may if he so desires given an address in India to which communications relating to the application may be sent). (see rule 19). Where the applicant has neither a place of business nor of residence in India the fact should be stated and an address for service in India given along with his address in his home country abroad.
5. Strike out if the mark is already in use
6. Strike out the words if not applicable. If user by predecessor(s) in title is claimed, the name(s) of such person(s) together with the date of commencement of use by the applicant himself should be stated at 8.
7. If there has been no use of the trade mark in respect of all the goods or services specified at 2, the items of goods or services in respect of which the mark has actually been used should be stated.
8. For additional matter if required, otherwise to be left blank .
9. If colour combination is claimed, clearly indicate it and state the

   Colour. If the application is in respect of a three dimensional mark, a statement to that effect (see rule 25 and 29).

10. Signature of the applicant or of his agent (legal practitioner or registered trade marks agent or person in the sole and regular employment of the applicant- See Section 145)

11. State the name of the place of the appropriate office of the Trade Marks Registry (see rule 4)

FORM TM-2

THE TRADE MARKS ACT, 1999

Agent's code No:

Proprietor's code No:

Fee: Rs.2500/-

Application for the registration of a trade mark (other than a collective mark or a certificate trade mark) in the Register from a convention country.

Section 18(1), 154(2). rule 25(3) and 26,

(To be filled in triplicate accompanied by five additional representation of the trade mark)

One representation to be fixed within this space and five others to be sent separately. Representation of the larger size may be folded but must then be mounted upon linen or other suitable material affixed thereto.(See rule 28).

Application is hereby made for registration in the register of the accompanying

trade mark in class [1] .... in respect of [2] ....in the name(s) of

[3].................. whose address is [4] .... who claim (s) to be the proprietor(s) thereof [and by whom the said mark is proposed to be used [5] or (and by whom and his (their) predecessor(s) in title [6] the said mark has been continuously used since ....] in respect of the said goods or services.7

The application in a convention country to register the trade mark has been made in on

A certified copy certified by an official of the convention country in which the application was filed is enclosed (along with its translation in English).

I/We request that the trade mark may be registered with priority date based on the above mentioned application in a convention country under the provisions of Section 154 of the Act.

8.................................. [9].................................

All communications relating to this application may be sent to the following address in India:-

Dated this ....day of ....20............

[10]..SIGNATURE

NAME OF SIGNATORY IN LETTERS.

To

The Registrar of Trade marks,

The office of the Trade Marks Registry at[11]........................

1. The Registrar's direction may be obtained if the class of the goods or services is not known.
2. Specify the goods or services for the class in respect of which application is made. A separate sheet detailing the goods or services may be used. The specification of goods or services should not ordinarily exceed five hundred characters. An excess space fee of Rs.10 per character is payable beyond this limit. See rule 25(16) The applicant shall state the exact number of excess characters where the specification of goods or services exceeds of five hundred characters at the space provided immediately before the signature.
3. Insert legibly the full name, description (occupation, calling and nationality of the applicant). In the case of a body corporate or firm the country of incorporation or the names and descriptions of the partners composing the firm and the nature of registration, if any, as the case may be, should be stated. (See rule 16).
4. The applicant shall state the address of his principal place of business in India, if any. (See rules 3 and 17) If the applicant carries on business in the goods or services for which registration is sought at only one place in India such fact should be stated and the address of the place given. If the applicant carries on business in the goods or services concerned at more places than one in India the applicant should state such fact and give the address of that place of business which he considers to be his principal place of business. If, however, the applicant does not carry on business in the goods or services concerned but carries on business in other goods or services at any one place in India this fact should be stated and the address of that place given; and where the applicant carries on such business at more places than one in India such fact should be stated and the address of the place which he considers to be his principal place of business given. Where the applicant is not carrying on any business in India the fact should be stated and the place of his residence in India, if any, should be stated and the address of that place given. In addition to the principal place of business or of residence in India, as the case may be, an applicant may if he so desires given an address in India to which communications relating to the application may be sent). (see rule 19). Where the applicant has neither a place of business nor of residence in India the fact should be stated and an address for service in India given along with his address in his home country abroad.
5. Strike out if the mark is already in use
6. Strike out the words if not applicable. If user by predecessor(s) in title is claimed the name(s) of such person(s) together with the date of commencement of use by the applicant himself should be stated at 8.
7. If there has been no use of the trade mark in respect of all the goods or services specified at 2, the items of goods or services in respect of which the mark has actually been used should be stated.
8. For additional matter if required, otherwise to be left blank .
9. If colour combination is claimed, clearly indicate it and state the

   Colour. If the application is in respect of a three dimensional mark, statement to that effect (see rule 25 and 29).

10. Signature of the applicant or of his agent (legal practitioner or registered trade marks agent or person in the sole and regular employment of the applicant- See Section 145).
11. State the name of the place of the appropriate office of the Trade Marks Registry – (See rule 4)

FORM TM-3

THE TRADE MARKS ACT, 1999

Agent's code No:

Proprietor's code No:

Fee Rs.10,000/-

Application for registration of a collective trade mark.

Section 63(1), rule 25(7) (a)and 128(1)

(To be filed in triplicate and accompanied by five representation of the collective mark and three copies of the draft regulation in Form **TM-49**).

One representation to be fixed within this space and four others to be sent separately. Representation of a larger size may be folded but must then be mounted upon linen or other suitable material and affixed hereto: (see rule 28).

Application is hereby made for registration in the register of the accompanying collective trade mark in class[1] ....in respect of[2] ....in the name of [3] .... whose address is [4] ....

All communications relating to this application may be sent to the following address in India:-

Dated this ....day of ....20.......

[5] ....

SIGNATURE

NAME OF SIGNATORY

To

The Registrar of Trade Marks,

The Office of the Trade Marks Registry at [6]

1. Registrar's direction may be obtained if the class is not known.

2. Specify the goods or services for the class in respect of which application is made. A separate sheet detailing the goods or services may be used. The specification of goods or services should not ordinarily exceed five hundred characters. An excess space fee of Rs.10 per character is payable beyond this limit. See rule 25(16) The applicant shall state the exact number of excess characters where the specification of goods or services exceeds of five hundred characters at the space provided immediately before the signature.
3. Insert the full name, description (occupation, calling and nationality) of the applicant. If the applicant is a body corporate, the nature and country of incorporation should be stated. (See Rule 16).

4. Here insert the full address of the applicant. [Address of the principal place of business or of residence in India, if any or address for service in India together with the address in the home country abroad].

5. Signature of the applicant or of his agent [legal practitioner or registered trade marks agent or person in the sole and regular employment of the applicant. (See Section 145)].

6. State the name of the place of the appropriate office of the Trade Marks Registry-(See rule 4).